ISBN 978-1-331-58617-3
PIBN 10209255

1 MONTH OF
FREE
READING

at
www.ForgottenBooks.com

By purchasing this book you are eligible for one month membership to ForgottenBooks.com, giving you unlimited access to our entire collection of over 700,000 titles via our web site and mobile apps.

To claim your free month visit:

www.forgottenbooks.com/free209255

Similar Books Are Available from
www.forgottenbooks.com

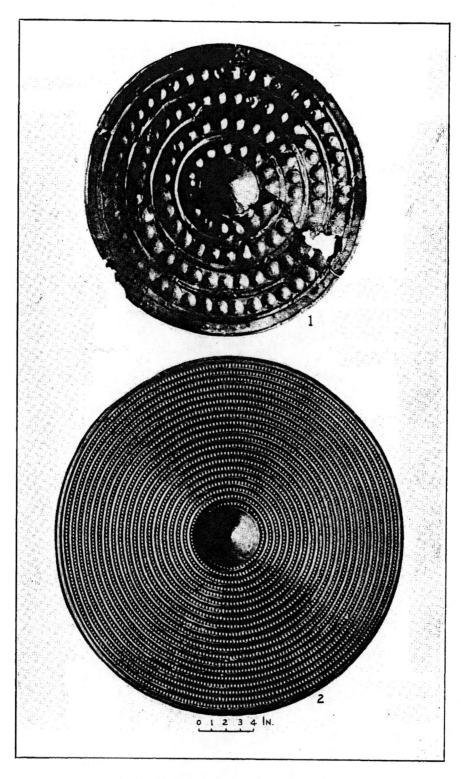

PLATE 1. BRONZE BUCKLERS, THAMES AND WALES.
(Cases 3–7, *see* p. 30.)

BRITISH MUSEUM

A GUIDE
TO THE ANTIQUITIES OF
THE BRONZE AGE

IN THE DEPARTMENT OF BRITISH
AND MEDIÆVAL ANTIQUITIES

WITH TEN PLATES AND 148 ILLUSTRATIONS

OXFORD
PRINTED AT THE UNIVERSITY PRESS
BY HORACE HART
PRINTER TO THE UNIVERSITY

PREFACE

As a sequel to the *Stone Age Guide*, published in 1902, the present volume is intended primarily to direct attention to our national antiquities, and to illustrate the connection between this country and the Continent in prehistoric times. For England, at least, there exists no work on the Bronze period that embraces the whole field, or brings the light of recent discoveries to bear upon Britain.

Considerable space has been necessarily devoted to the description of remains in England, but it is hoped that the treatment of certain areas abroad, of greater importance in themselves, will not be found too condensed. Much that was formerly regarded as vaguely prehistoric is now seen to belong to well-ascertained stages in the development of the highest ancient civilisations, and the objects themselves belong more properly to the Egyptian and Assyrian or to the Greek and Roman department. For this reason only typical series of such remains can be shown in the Prehistoric Room. Most of the antiquities here belong undoubtedly to the Bronze age, but there must have been a considerable overlap at the beginning and end of the period. Reference is made to certain stone and other primitive implements that clearly survived into the age of metal, and a compromise has been arrived at with regard to the Early Iron age. Bronze relics of what is known as the Hallstatt period are exhibited in this Room and included in the Guide, while those of iron, in many cases contemporary, are reserved for future treatment.

The collections from the British Isles in the Museum are fairly complete, but it is unfortunate that remains from Ireland, the district richest in gold and bronze antiquities of the period, should so seldom have a history: even when the locality is recorded, the circumstances of the discovery are generally unknown. It is in this way that prehistoric archaeology is thwarted at every turn; and one need only look at the Danish national antiquities to appreciate the value of some official control over early remains found in the soil.

In the work of arranging and describing the bronzes, Sir John Evans' comprehensive and laborious work has been of great service ; and for the barrows of this country, Canon Greenwell's book on the subject has been largely drawn upon. Special mention must also be made of Prof. Montelius' classification for various parts of Europe: his beautifully illustrated works are generally regarded as of high authority. The opinions of other eminent archaeologists, at home and abroad, have also been frequently cited ; while Prof. Gowland of the Royal College of Science, Prof. Rhŷs of Oxford, and Canon Greenwell of Durham have very kindly read in proof the passages dealing with subjects on which they are recognised authorities.

The Trustees are indebted to one of their number, Sir John Evans, for the loan of figs. 15, 33, 34, 35, 51, 53, 57, 58, 98 and 112; to the Council of the Society of Antiquaries for figs. 17, 22, 23, 45, 71, 93, 94, 96, 97, 124 and 145 ; and to the Delegates of the Oxford University Press for permission to use figs. 1, 2, 29–32, 36, 37 and 88, originally published in Canon Greenwell's *British Barrows*. Where the illustrations are not full size, the amount of reduction is generally indicated by a fraction ; thus, ½ means that the original has twice the length and breadth, but four times the area, of the reproduction.

The term *millennium* has been occasionally adopted for any of the successive periods of 1000 years before our era ; for example, the first Egyptian dynasty is assigned to the middle of the fifth millennium (about 4500 B.C.), and the siege of Troy is generally supposed to have taken place towards the close of the second millennium (about 1100 B.C.). In describing the Table-Cases it has been found desirable to speak of the west and east sides, and of the left and right sections of either. To facilitate reference a plan of the room, giving the cardinal points, is provided on the back cover of the Guide.

CHARLES H. READ.

CONTENTS

LIST OF PLATES

LIST OF ILLUSTRATIONS

INTRODUCTION

ONE of the most important steps in human progress is marked by the introduction of metal. Apart from the invention of fire-making, which in the childhood of the race helped to raise man above the lower animals, there has been no such advance in our material condition until the development of steam and electricity in quite recent years. The enormous period known as the Stone age, which can only be measured by geological time, left man still ignorant of many essential arts of life. Substantial progress there had certainly been, as the scanty relics of that time demonstrate; but it was in many particulars insignificant in comparison with the results achieved since metal superseded stone some 5,000 or 6,000 years ago. The earliest efforts of the worker in metal, which made such rapid progress possible, are therefore of transcendent importance in the history of civilisation.

The period from the beginning of metallurgy down to the dawn of recorded history is commonly divided into two parts, named after the metals which successively occupied the most prominent place in human industry: an earlier or 'Bronze age,' and a later age of Iron. These terms are so convenient that they have passed into general use, but it must be remembered that no two prehistoric periods can be separated by a hard and fast line. As stated in the preface to the *Guide to the Antiquities of the Stone Age*, the words do not denote divisions of time, but stages of human culture which gradually supersede each other and are not uniform in all parts of the world. The object of the present Guide is to give a general idea of the Bronze age in its various developments, as illustrated by the Museum Collections. While it has been sometimes necessary, for the better comprehension of the Bronze age as a whole, to treat of parts of the world almost unrepresented in the Prehistoric Room, a proportionately greater space has been devoted to those countries which have furnished larger series of objects, or which stand in a necessary relation to the early archaeology of Britain. To the antiquities of these islands an exceptional position has naturally been assigned.

The very use of the term Bronze age may appear to beg a serious question, for though bronze was undoubtedly the most important metal employed in the early period, it was probably not the first to be fashioned into an implement or a weapon. There are two other metals, copper and iron, in favour of which a claim for priority has been put forward, and of their respective claims a few words must necessarily be said. Metallurgists have pointed out that there is no reason in the nature of things why *iron* should not have first attracted some inventive genius at the close of the neolithic age. Its ores are more abundant and more easily reduced than any others, while in its meteoric form it requires no reduction at all. In this form it has within the memory of man been fashioned into implements by the Eskimo of Greenland, probably without any suggestion or aid from foreign peoples; and it is reasonable to inquire whether it may not have occurred in a similar way and been similarly used in other parts of the world at a very remote epoch. It has been suggested, for example, that the use of iron might have been easily discovered by the accidental reduction of a rich piece of ore on the domestic hearth, and the way thus opened to an experimental repetition of the process. It should further be remembered that iron may have been known in Egypt almost, if not quite, as early as bronze; that is to say, as early as the fourth and sixth dynasties. A piece of iron dating from the fourth dynasty is exhibited in the Third Egyptian Room (Case K 29, No. 2433); while a fragment of hydrated oxide from the sixth, recently discovered by Prof. Petrie, is shown in Case J (p. 126). These finds confirm literary evidence on the importance of which Egyptologists have long insisted. The word for iron occurs in the Pyramid texts of Unas, and in the paintings of the time of the Ancient Empire weapons and tools are painted blue or black, the hues in which this metal is always represented. Iron plays a prominent part in ancient Egyptian myths, the firmament of heaven being described as a rectangular iron plate; and its Egyptian name is *báa-en-pet*, 'metal of heaven,' evidently in allusion to the meteoric form in which it may first have been known. The Chinese too are thought to have been acquainted with iron at least as early as 1000 B.C., and probably even earlier, the province of Shan Si having certainly been productive of the metal since very remote times. But reasonable as such arguments in favour of the priority of iron may appear in themselves, there is one thing wanting to their serious consideration: they are not often borne out by archaeological discovery. We know that when men have once become acquainted with the harder metal, they soon cease to make their weapons of the softer; the fact is proved beyond controversy by finds of the transition period at the close of the Bronze age, when the bronze sword or dagger is superseded by that of iron, bronze being retained only for ceremonial or ornamental purposes. It is most unlikely that if iron had been used before any other metal, it should have fallen into disuse in any place where its ores could readily be obtained; or that men once acquainted with its superior merit should have continued to manufacture weapons of a metal inferior in offensive power. This consideration disposes of the argument that primaeval iron weapons may once have existed but have now rusted away; for it is not to be supposed that the long series of bronze weapons which we now possess would ever have been made if all the time iron had lain ready to the hands of their makers. It is equally difficult to believe that iron weapons deposited with the dead should have disappeared so completely as to have left in no single instance even a trace of discoloration upon the surrounding objects. The following remarks of Sir John Evans, which have a direct bearing upon this subject, may fitly be quoted here: 'When barrow after barrow is opened, and weapons of bronze and stone only are found accompanying the interments, and not a trace of iron or steel; when hoards of rough metal and broken bronze, together with the moulds of the bronze-founder and some of his stock-in-trade, are disinterred, and there is no trace of an iron tool among them— the presumption is strong that at the time when these men and these hoards were buried, iron was not in use. When, moreover, by a careful examination of the forms of bronze instruments we can trace a certain amount of development which is in keeping with the peculiar properties of bronze, and not with those of iron, and we can thus to some extent fix a kind of chronological succession in these forms, the inference is that this evolution of form, which must have required a considerable amount of time, took place without its course being affected by any introduction of a fresh and qualifying influence in the shape of iron tools and weapons. When, however, in various countries we find interments and even cemeteries in which bronze and iron weapons and instruments are intermingled, and the forms of those in bronze are what we have learned from other sources to regard as the latest, while the forms in iron are not those for which that metal is best adapted, but are almost servile copies of the bronze instruments found with them, the proof of the one having succeeded the other is almost absolutely conclusive.'

The same authority points out that at Hallstatt and other places in which graves have been examined belonging to the transitional period, when both iron and bronze were in' use together, the weapons and tools of iron, though oxidised, still retain their form and character as completely as those in bronze. This fact affords strong ground for believing that had iron been present with bronze in other early interments, it would also have been preserved. Arguments like these are incontrovertible in the case of most countries where prehistoric implements have been found, but in such regions as north-eastern Africa there is still perhaps room for doubt. Evidence in favour of the extreme antiquity of iron in Egypt has already been given, and it must not be forgotten that Africa, which as a continent never had a Bronze age, was possessed of abundant ores from which good malleable iron could be extracted by processes far simpler than those required for the manufacture of bronze. The district west of the Upper Nile is very rich in iron, and Professor Gowland has shown that the furnace used in modern times in Kordofan has close analogies with one represented on a tomb bearing the name of Thothmes III (about 1530 B.C.) and with those employed by the Etruscans and other peoples of Southern Europe west of the Apennines. The metallurgy of iron in this part of Africa was evidently both an ancient and a vigorous art, and its origins may be more remote than is usually suspected.

Iron may, however, be fairly eliminated from the general inquiry: there remain copper and bronze, the former a simple metal, the latter an alloy of copper and tin. In Alaska, about the Coppermine River, and on the shores of Lake Superior in North America, and in parts of Central Africa, ores containing copper in the metallic state were made by the natives into knives and spear-heads before the advent of the European invader, and some of the American tribes thus passed from the exclusive use of stone to the knowledge of copper simply by the exercise of their own inventive faculty. If the Red Indian was able to make this advance, why, it may be asked, should not prehistoric man have done the same in Europe? But the North American copper ores contained nodules and large masses of copper as metal, and were treated by the Indians as if they had been stone, being hammered into shape without exposure to heat: the Indians were thus merely users of metal and in no sense metallurgists. On the other hand, the prehistoric inhabitants of the Old World melted their copper before they fashioned it; at any rate all the copper implements known to science have certainly been produced by casting, which presupposes a more significant advance in human knowledge, and one much more difficult to explain, involving as it does the introduction of completely new methods and the employment of fire. In some localities where oxidised copper ores (cuprite or malachite) occur in admixture with tin ore (cassiterite), a true bronze may have been made contemporaneously with, or even earlier than, the pure metal; and the alloy, at first due to accident, may have been almost immediately reproduced of set purpose. For the primitive mind is not unobservant, and if many of the uncivilised tribes of the modern world are capable of the like simple experimental processes, there is no reason why prehistoric man should not have given proof of similar aptitude. But it is probable that in most localities copper was really the first metal of which implements were made, and, being far more widely distributed than tin (the second constituent of bronze), is more likely to have attracted man's notice first, especially in the form of oxides and carbonates, which are surface ores. There are still great numbers of primitive metal implements which have not been chemically analysed, and the material available for a scientific generalisation is very incomplete; but the evidence so far as it goes is against a *universal* stage of culture characterised by the sole use of copper. Such a stage is not proved, for instance, in Britain, though certain indications seem to point in that direction. The fact that the most primitive forms frequently prove to be made of copper, though favourable to the theory of a Copper age, is not in itself conclusive; for, as the opponents of the theory have pointed out, copper can only be successfully cast in flat moulds open to the air, and if it is poured into double or closed moulds it produces unsatisfactory results. Even if all the known implements of primitive form proved to be of copper, this might still only show that tin was for some reason temporarily unobtainable, and that casters who were perfectly well able to produce forms of a more elaborate description, fell back on the forms of primitive appearance because these were alone suited to the metal actually at their disposal. Really effective evidence in favour of a general phase of culture based on the exclusive employment of copper, though it may confirm the argument from form, must be independent of it, and such independence can only be claimed in certain definite regions such as the countries of the Eastern Mediterranean. Over this area the occurrence of copper in deposits unquestionably older than the first appearance of bronze, is too frequent to be accounted for on the supposition of a temporary failure of tin; and though the conditions were not quite the same in Europe, the analysis of various specimens has shown that a similar state of affairs may have existed in some parts of our own continent. In many districts of Europe, indeed, such as North Italy and Hungary, analysis is in favour of a primitive copper culture, while in Ireland the results as yet obtained seem to tell the same tale. The presence of a small percentage of tin—anything from 0·5 to 1 or even 2 per cent.—need not imply an intentional addition, because the impure ores from which the implements were made have been shown to contain the same admixture: the tin was in these cases not added by man with the object of hardening the metal, and consequently the implements are copper, and not a poor quality of bronze. Such natural admixtures are most frequent, and offer the highest percentage of tin, in areas where tin ores also occur; but they are also found in districts where tin ore has never yet been found, for instance at Campos and Parazuelos in south-eastern Spain. The same remarks apply to arsenic and antimony, which are also common impurities of copper ore and have a like hardening effect. Mr. George Coffey, in discussing the composition of primitive Irish celts, has fairly argued that 'only when it has been shown that the local ores, from which it may be presumed that the copper was obtained, are free from tin, does it seem allowable to argue that the tin has been added, and even then the possibility that the copper or implements were imported has to be considered.' In some cases, as for example in Babylonia, the evidence for the priority of copper may be described as stratigraphical, and is in no way dependent upon primitive appearance.

If then we assume that copper preceded bronze in many parts of the world, we may suppose that progress was effected very much on the following lines. In a favoured district, or possibly in more than one place about the same time, a simple process of moulding molten copper as a substitute for stone may have been suggested by an accident, such as the partial melting of a piece of surface ore in the hearth. The new material was found convenient for several reasons, notably because it was not brittle, and because a number of implements could be made with rapidity from a single mould. But in many respects it proved inferior to the stone which preceded it, for if the ore was pure it was extremely soft, and its cutting edge was easily dulled; it became necessary therefore to find some means of hardening the metal. Probably by experiment the inhabitants of some region in which not only copper but also tin occurred, discovered that copper could be most effectively hardened by the addition of tin. They would transmit the alloy to their neighbours; and by degrees, following the great lines of commerce and intercourse, first its use and ultimately its manufacture would become known to almost all the peoples of the ancient world. Those who had already experimented with copper would immediately adopt the superior alloy; those who were still in the neolithic stage would pass without transition to the use of bronze. It cannot be affirmed as a universal rule that the proportion of tin alloy in the early bronzes only reached the ratio of about 10 per cent. by a slow and gradual advance. It is indeed a plausible theory that the most ancient specimens are the poorest in tin, and that as this metal grew more plentiful the alloy became richer by degrees, but there are facts which tell in the opposite direction. In the second city of Hissarlik, for instance, which preceded the Homeric city of Troy by about a thousand years, a bronze very rich in tin makes its appearance suddenly, without having been preceded by poorer alloys (p. 119). In concluding these remarks upon the order in which metals were used, we may draw attention to some of the literary evidence proving that the ancient traditions as to the sequence of prehistoric ages have often been confirmed by modern archaeology. Hesiod, in his *Works and Days*, speaks of a time when men wrought in bronze, but when 'dark iron was unknown.' And Lucretius in the fifth book of his poem on the *Nature of the Universe* gives a graphic picture of primitive life, towards the close of which occurs the distinct statement that iron (*ferrum*) was discovered later than *aes* (copper?). Again, Aeschylus in his tragedy of the *Seven against Thebes* alludes to iron as the 'stranger from across the sea,' 'the new-comer from the Scythians,' and 'the Chalybian stranger,' the two last expressions pointing to the eastern shores of the Black Sea as one of the sources from which the Greeks obtained their iron. Here under the shadow of the Caucasus and not far from the Scythian steppes lived the Chalybes, one of the great iron-working peoples of the Old World, whose name has been transmitted through the adjective 'chalybeate' to the modern languages of Europe. These allusions of Aeschylus point to a time when iron was still regarded somewhat as an intruder, and illustrate the super-stitious feeling of almost all peoples who have passed from one stage of culture into another. Compared with the newer metal, the old has a prestige and sanctity attaching to it, as having been associated from ancient times with the gods and heroes of their race. Allusion has been made to a similar feeling in favour of stone in the *Stone Age Guide*, where instances were mentioned of stone knives being still used for ceremonial purposes long after the knowledge of bronze had become general. We find the same veneration for the implements of older times in the later period when bronze had in its turn been superseded by iron. In ancient Rome the priest of Jupiter might shave his beard only with a bronze knife, and it was an ancient usage that the site of a new town might only be ploughed round with a ploughshare made of bronze. The same feeling is expressed in the Book of Deuteronomy (xxvii. 5): 'And there thou shalt build an altar to the Lord thy God, an altar of stones: thou shalt not lift up any iron upon them.' Folklore tells a con-stant tale of the fear with which iron was everywhere regarded as something new and uncanny by the conservative sentiment of the countryside, a fear engendering a feeling of awe for the smiths and founders who were able to bend the formidable substance to their will. To the smiths mysterious powers were generally assigned, and they were often regarded as abnormal or even supernatural beings. Sir Walter Scott in *Kenilworth* has utilised the legend of Wayland Smith, the northern hero of the forge; while Greek and Roman mythology places a metal-worker, Hephaestus or Vulcan, among the gods. His workshops were held to be in the volcanic districts of Sicily and the neighbouring islands; and here, in the caverns beneath Etna, the Cyclops forged the armour which Thetis begged for her son Achilles before he sailed for the siege of Troy. Even the representatives of a despised or vanquished people have reaped the advantage of this sentiment if, as has sometimes happened, the dominant race is less skilled in the working of metals.

It now becomes necessary to touch upon another unsolved

problem, the origin of the manufacture of bronze. In what part of the world was the alloy first produced? Any answer given to this question must necessarily take into consideration the distribution of tin; for if traces of tin workings exist within easy reach of the most ancient centres of civilisation, a way out of the difficulty might be found. At present the piece of bronze for which the highest antiquity is claimed is the rod found at Mêdûm in Egypt, dating from 3700 B.C. Mesopotamia can show a bronze statuette of Gudea (2500 B.C.), and an almost contemporary bronze vase of Ur Gur; and as their manufacture presupposes a considerable metallurgical skill, the first acquaintance of the Chaldaeans with bronze may go back to an even earlier date than that at which the alloy became known to the Egyptians. But so far as is known, tin was not found within the borders either of Egypt or Babylonia; and the nearest regions rich in metals, even Armenia and the Caucasus, appear to be devoid of stanniferous ores. Tin is said to exist in Asia Minor, and the Greek historian Strabo declares that it was produced in Drangiana, west of the modern Afghanistan, a district partly coinciding with Khorassan, where its presence has been confirmed. It is also found in other parts of Persia, near Asterabad and Tabriz, and the allusion to it in Numbers xxxi as part of the spoils of Midian, suggests that there may even have been mines in north-west Arabia. From such sources as these the tin used in casting the earliest bronze may have been derived, but it must be confessed that we are here in a region of conjecture where probability has to take the place of evidence. In Eastern Asia, beyond the radius of the ancient civilisations of Mesopotamia, there would seem to be no region likely to have witnessed the discovery nearer than Southern China; for India, which has copper implements of a very primitive type, is poor in tin, her so-called bronze being often really brass; while the Malay peninsula, an extremely rich stanniferous region, does not appear to have been mined in very ancient times. In Southern China copper and tin are found together in abundance under conditions which would give every opportunity for primitive experiment; but here again we have to rest content with a bare statement of possibility, for proofs are not forthcoming. We know nothing of the state of China in the fifth millennium B.C.; yet unless a theory of independent invention in different parts of the world is adopted, it is to this remote period that the first use of bronze in that country must be assigned. If China originated, Mesopotamia and

Egypt must have followed, and yet they have produced bronze nearly as early as 4000 B.C. And the difficulty would hardly be lessened if the date of the Mêdûm rod should prove to be a thousand years later than that usually claimed for it, since our knowledge of the fourth millennium in China is no greater than it is of the fifth. The search for the birthplace of bronze in China is therefore barren of positive results, though there is ample room for future discovery in what is, archaeologically speaking, still an unknown land. The East thus affording no certain clue, the possibilities of the West may be briefly examined. Tin is found in Britain, France, north-west Spain, Italy, Germany, Bohemia, and the Balkan Peninsula, mostly within reach of copper ores. Here, however, we are once more confronted by the difficulty that proofs of the invention are lacking, and that unless we suppose more than one centre of discovery, the acceptance of a European claim to priority would imply a knowledge of bronze in the West as early as 4000 B.C., or, if the Mêdûm rod should prove untrustworthy, a thousand years later. But though in after times Egypt drew her supplies of tin from Europe, it would be bold indeed to suppose that she did so even at the more recent of these two dates, and still bolder to maintain that she learned from northern peoples how to make the alloy called bronze. In the present state of our knowledge we are unable to solve these problems, and if the attribution of the discovery to Babylonia is preferred as offering fewest difficulties, it must be regarded as little more than a temporary hypothesis. It is of course conceivable that there may after all have been more than one centre of invention; for if such an independent discovery took place in America, as some authorities hold, (p. 110), it might equally well have done so both in Asia and Europe. But there is much to be said against this view; and if the forms of our dolmens and chambered tombs of the neolithic period are of oriental derivation, while Mediterranean influence crossed the Alps and the Danube at almost as early a time, there is certainly a presumption that the art of casting bronze in Europe was equally dependent on the Nearer East. Wherever bronze may have first been made, its obvious 'superiority over copper and stone caused it to be adopted by all peoples who could procure either the manufactured alloy or the tin which would enable them to produce it for themselves. Its use spread with comparative rapidity from end to end of the ancient world; and as this vast area provided ample room for the development of local types, it is natural to find a number of archaeological provinces, overlapping each other at certain points, but distinguished by marked individual peculiarities. Thus the style of Western Europe differs from that of Scandinavia and North Germany; the lake-dwellings of Central Europe have a common culture; Italy, the Balkan Peninsula and the Danube valley, are more closely related to the countries of the south-eastern Mediterranean; the Islands of the Aegean have more points of contact with Asia Minor, Egypt, and the early civilisation of the Nearer East; while the immense area extending from South Russia across the Ural Mountains and the Altai Range is in touch with the western frontiers of China. Within these provinces there are various subdivisions affected by special geographical and cultural conditions, which will be mentioned below in the short introductions to particular countries. In the present place only a few general considerations can be introduced which may help to explain why the Bronze culture often shows markedly different types in districts not very far removed from each other.

It has been stated in the *Stone Age Guide* (p. xii) that there is no sharp line of demarcation between the great prehistoric periods, and that some regions received and developed new inventions far earlier than others. The important step of discarding bronze in favour of iron was taken by some peoples centuries earlier than others, although the distance between their territories may have been only a few hundred miles. The reason for this inequality of culture is to be sought in geographical conditions. Those countries which were situated upon or near the main lines of commerce and intercourse were naturally the first to take advantage of the latest achievements of human ingenuity, while those which lay in remote inaccessible parts of the world were content to continue for a long series of years the use of a material which had already been superseded among their more progressive neighbours. The loss in aggressive power by the more backward peoples through the continued use of a metal inferior to iron for warlike purposes was not without compensating advantages; for as the time during which they used bronze was indefinitely prolonged, they were able to develop the artistic qualities of the metal in a higher degree, and to produce more varied forms with ornamentation of more elaborate design. On the other hand, the bronze implements and weapons discovered in countries where iron was early introduced are in comparison scantier and less decorative, because there was less time for such a prolonged artistic development. Italy, Southern France, and Upper Austria all offer examples of a Bronze culture cut off before it reached full perfection, the former country having always been open to all the civilising influences of the Mediterranean, while Southern France and Upper Austria, lying as they did on the great trade-routes for tin and amber (p. 95), were naturally quick to adopt any useful innovation. In all these countries, therefore, bronze antiquities tend to be simpler and less ornate than in regions where the introduction of iron was delayed. Very different were the conditions in Eastern Hungary and Scandinavia. The first region lay away to the east of the amber route from the head of the Adriatic to the Baltic; while the second was the end of the known world, and was naturally the latest to be affected by southern civilisation. The consequence of this comparative isolation was in an artistic sense a happy one, for in these regions the Bronze age is represented by a series of antiquities which for splendour and wealth of ornament have no parallel among the remains of countries otherwise more favourably situated. Sentimental or religious reasons seem also to have intensified the conservatism natural to remote populations, for there is some reason to believe that the inhabitants of the less progressive countries at first adopted a rather hostile attitude to iron, and in their attachment to the more beautiful metal, to which they had been so long accustomed, were disposed to resist the introduction of an unfamiliar substitute.

The principal questions connected with the first appearance of metals in human industry having been thus briefly indicated, it is now desirable that something should be said about the peoples concerned with the early development of metallurgy. To attempt to deal with the ethnology of the whole ancient world at the period when metal-working first became general would be impossible here. The position and movements of the Eastern peoples will therefore be omitted, and the attention of the reader almost exclusively directed to the groups inhabiting those parts of the world with which the British Islands and the adjoining countries are most intimately connected.

Before the racial affinities of the primitive European population are considered, something must be said on the Aryan question, which has passed through several stages, but is not by any means finally settled. Towards the close of the eighteenth century, Sir William Jones drew attention to the striking similarities between Sanskrit, Greek, Latin, German, and Keltic, similarities that could only be explained by a common parentage. Bopp's *Comparative Grammar*, published in 1833–5, established the science of comparative philology; and all the European languages except Basque, Finnic, Magyar, and Turkish were comprised in what was called the Indo-Germanic group. The title is misleading, but the more usual term Aryan, invented by the late Professor Max Müller, is also open to many objections. *Arya* is a Sanskrit adjective meaning ' noble,' and in the Vedic hymns it appears to be a name assumed by the conquerors who introduced the language of the Vedas into India. In the Zendavesta, the most ancient Persian text, the country of the Aryans is mentioned, and it was long held that Ariana, the district round Herat, was the cradle of the Aryan languages. Professor Max Müller was the foremost champion in this country of the Asiatic origin of the Aryan civilisation, and in 1861 spoke not only of an Aryan language, but an Aryan race or family; this was originally settled on the Central Asian plateau, and spoke a language not yet Sanskrit, or Greek, or German, but containing the dialectical germs of all these kindred tongues. The conclusions as to the Aryan civilisation reached by extreme philologists are now greatly discredited, and the reaction against the oriental origin of the Aryan was started as early as 1851, when Dr. R. G. Latham, of Cambridge, published his objections to the prevalent theory. He pointed out that the bulk of the Aryan peoples is found in Europe, and only a detached body in Asia, while Lithuanian is closely related to Sanskrit, and no less archaic. The specially archaic character of Sanskrit and Zend is mainly due to the fact that documents in those languages happen to be older than those in any other Aryan tongue. If, for example, we possessed a Lithuanian literature of the same early date, it might with equal justice be argued that the cradle of the Aryans was in the neighbourhood of the Baltic. The philological evidence, so far as it goes, is against the view advocated by Professor Sayce in 1880, that the primeval Aryan community inhabited Bactriana, near the sources of the Oxus and Jaxartes. The question as to the distribution of the beech-tree is also important, and turns on the original meaning of the word represented in Greek by φηγός, and in Latin by *fagus*. It is common to all the Aryan languages of Europe, and is generally taken to indicate the beech, though in Greek it undoubtedly means the oak. This may be accounted for by the fact that the beech is not found in the Morea or south of the line between the Gulf of Arta and the Malian Gulf, where the oak flourishes; and the ancestors of the Greeks on reaching the peninsula from the Balkans may have transferred the name.   Nor does the beech occur east of a line drawn from the southern extremities of Norway and Sweden, through Königsberg, east of Poland along the Bug Valley, to the Crimea and the Caucasus.   This is so far in favour of an European origin for the Aryan language, if not for an Aryan race, and though the claims of Scandinavia have been brought prominently forward by Karl Penka and others, south-west Russia seems to be the district open to least objection.

This will become more apparent when a sketch has been given of the civilisation reached by the Aryans before their dispersion.   A study of their vocabulary, such as that undertaken by Dr. Schrader, and edited for English readers by Principal Jevons, shows that in their original home they had reached a stage of culture that is best illustrated by the earliest remains discovered in the lake-dwellings of Switzerland.   According to the late Canon Taylor, they were nomad herdsmen who had domesticated the dog, and possessed ox-wagons and dug-out canoes, but no metals except possibly copper.   During summer they lived in huts, during winter in pits.   Their dress consisted of skins sewn together, and they knew how to kindle fire and to count up to 100.   It is doubtful whether they tilled the ground, but they probably pounded wild cereals, such as spelt and barley, in stone mortars.   Marriage was a recognised institution, but they were polygamists, and practised human sacrifice.   While believing in a future life, as is shown by their care of the dead, they had no idols, but probably reverenced the powers of nature.   In the way of food they had hazel-nuts, water-chestnuts, and acorns, but it is remarkable that they did not habitually eat fish.   No common word for any kind of fish has survived in their language, with one or two possible exceptions.   In this connection it may be mentioned that the Homeric heroes regarded fish as starvation diet, and Herodotus uses 'fish-eater' as a term of reproach; while to judge from the huge refuse-heaps known as kitchen-middens, the earliest inhabitants of Scandinavia lived on little else but fish, and for this and other reasons cannot be regarded as a branch of the Aryan family.

Strictly speaking, the term Aryan should be only applied

to the primitive people who evolved the root-words and grammatical forms that can be traced in Greek, Latin, and other Italian or Romance languages, Celtic, Teutonic, Slavonic, Lithuanic or Lettic, and Albanian; in fourteen modern Indian languages derived from Sanskrit; in Zend, Persian, Pushtu or Afghan, Baluchi, Kurdish and Ossetic; and in Armenian. It must, however, be borne in mind that only a small pro- portion of the millions who speak these languages can possibly represent an original Aryan people, nor is community of lan- guage an argument for blood-relationship. The opinion is becoming more and more general that the Aryan language was forced upon the aboriginal inhabitants of Europe towards the end of the neolithic period; and this was due to invasion by a stalwart race with short skulls and fair hair, who radiated from some point in south-east Europe into the Mediterranean peninsulas, into France, Germany, and Britain. The new-comers are sometimes known as the Alpine race, and seem to have settled in strength along the Upper Danube and in Switzerland. Some authorities regard the Kelts as the most direct descendants of the primitive Aryan stock, while the other peoples who speak Aryan dialects are of impure descent, and were only Aryanised by conquest.

And here some explanation of the term Kelt is necessary. It is throughout spelt in this way to prevent any possibility of confusion with the celt, an implement of chisel-form (from an imaginary Latin word *celtis*), of which specimens both in stone and bronze are exhibited in this gallery. A far more subtle danger lies in the common confusion of the Kelts of philology and the Kelts of history and ethnology; and although it would be impossible to restrict the term to one or the other application, the following table will show the many differences that exist between those who speak or spoke the Keltic language in these islands, and those who trace their descent from the Kelts of Caesar's time:—

KELTS OF PHILOLOGY.	KELTS OF HISTORY.
Represented in Britain by the Gaels and Brythons (known later as the Kymry or Welsh), who are the people of the Round-barrows, tall, with hair probably reddish, moderately brachycephalic, with a mean cephalic index of 81.	Located in Central France, the *Gallia Celtica* of Caesar; and represented by the inhabi- tants of Auvergne, Dauphiny, Savoy, the Grisons and Mari- time Alps: short, dark-haired, and extremely brachycephalic, with a mean cephalic index of 84.

Kelt is therefore a misnomer if applied to either of the two races in our islands by whom Keltic is spoken, either the tall, red-haired, mesaticephalic Irishman and Scot, or the short, dark, dolichocephalic race of South Wales, which has been traced by some in Ireland. There is indeed a bond of union between the Kelts of philology and history, inasmuch as the people of Central Gaul in Caesar's time spoke a Keltic language, but this was probably forced upon them by the southern expansion of the Belgic Gauls with whom our Kymry and Gaels are ethnologically connected.

Something may now be said of the traces left by the inhabitants of this country during the Bronze age. The barrows of Britain have occupied the attention of many eminent archaeologists; and the broad results of their exploration may here be mentioned, though it cannot be pretended that any great uniformity has been observed, or that the deductions drawn are in any way final.

First, as to the disposal of the dead. In the neolithic period, to which the Long barrows are referred, we meet with a striking difference in the methods adopted in the north and south of England. While an elaborate system of cremation was adopted in Yorkshire and Westmorland, the Long barrows of Wiltshire and Gloucestershire contained unburnt burials, but there are at the same time points of uniformity which indicate that the difference was one of locality only and not of date; for the skulls are uniformly long (dolichocephalic), and the barrows themselves are very long in comparison with their breadth, and almost always placed with their long diameter east and west, while the primary interment is generally at the east end, which is both broader and higher than the other.

In the Bronze age, both burnt and unburnt burials are found in barrows that are circular and more or less conical; and instances may be quoted in which the circumstances show that both methods were resorted to on certain occasions: for instance, in a mound on Acklam Wold, Yorkshire, opened in 1849, a pile of burnt bones was in close contact with the legs of a skeleton buried in the usual contracted position, and they seemed to have been deposited while yet hot, for the knees of the skeleton were completely charred. It has been suggested that in cases like this, or where an unburnt body is surrounded by a ring of urn-burials (as fig. 28), the entire skeletons may be those of chiefs or heads of families, and the burnt bones those of slaves, dependants, or even wives, sacrificed at the funeral. The practice of *suttee* in Europe rests indeed on the authority of Julius Caesar, who represents such religious suicides as having, at no remote period from his own, formed a part of the funeral rites of the Gaulish chiefs; and also states that the relatives of a deceased chieftain accused his wives of being accessory to his death, and often tortured them to death on that account.

Details of burials in Round barrows will be found in the description of the cases containing pottery and other remains from these sources (pp. 42–64); but the excavations and publications of Sir Richard Colt Hoare in Wiltshire, of Chas. Warne in Dorset, Thos. Bateman in Derbyshire, and Canon Greenwell and the Rev. J. C. Atkinson in Yorkshire and the north, have brought out some striking facts with regard to Bronze age interments in England. The results obtained before 1874 were ably summarised by Dr. Thurnam, who had himself excavated in Wiltshire and elsewhere; and the following points are derived from his voluminous paper on *Ancient British Barrows*, and from Canon Greenwell's book. While in Derbyshire, Staffordshire, and Yorkshire the unburnt burials slightly preponderated, in Wiltshire and Dorset they amount to less than a quarter of the total explored; though it must be observed that in Cleveland, the extreme north-east district of Yorkshire, the interments in forty grave-mounds excavated by Mr. Atkinson had been without exception by way of cremation. Cremation appears to have been by far the most common usage in Cornwall, and almost universal in the counties of Denbigh, Merioneth, and Carnarvon; while in Northumberland the proportion of burnt to unburnt bodies, from over seventy interments, was almost two to one. About one quarter of the cremated bodies in Wiltshire were deposited in cinerary urns, in striking contrast to what was observed in the adjoining county of Dorset, where the proportion is almost exactly the reverse, or as three to one. In Cleveland the burnt bones were collected in urns in thirty-two cases out of fifty, and in general it was noticed that urns were utilised much less frequently in the Yorkshire Wolds than in other parts of England, though there seems to have been nowhere any rule as to their upright or inverted position in the barrows.

The occurrence of bronze or copper implements and ornaments in the Round barrows has an important bearing on their date; and in this respect there are wide differences observable in various parts of the kingdom. It must be borne in mind that a large majority of the interments have no articles of any description associated with them, and many of the remainder have only pins, buttons, or other minor objects. The appearance of metal, usually bronze, is the important point, and this seems to be more frequent in the districts most easily accessible from the Continent. For instance, about one-fifth of the total interments, burnt and unburnt, explored by Hoare in Wilts., contained bronze implements, weapons, or ornaments; and only half as many contained objects of stone, which are presumptive evidence of earlier date or of inferior civilisation. In Derbyshire, on the contrary, interments accompanied by stone implements were nearly four times as frequent as those with bronze; while figures are given elsewhere (p. 57) showing that only about 4 per cent. of the interments on the Yorkshire Wolds contained metallic objects of any kind, against 17 per cent. with implements of stone. In the words of Dr. Thurnam, the inference need not be that there is any great difference in the epoch to which the grave-mounds of the various districts are to be attributed; but rather that the southern tribes were better or earlier provided with bronze than the northern; and that the use of weapons and implements of this metal began on the southern coast, and thence gradually spread over the interior and north of the island.

In connection with the spread of bronze throughout this country, it should be mentioned that though there is a great variety in the hundreds of bronze implements discovered, either in hoards or scattered over the surface, sunk in boggy ground, or lying on a river-bed, a very small proportion of types has ever been found in barrows, either in association with interments or lying apart in the material of the mound. Those that have occurred in burial-mounds are comprised under the head of the plain axe or celt, the knife-dagger, drill, and awl; while swords, daggers of another kind, spearheads, the other types of celts, gouges, and chisels are conspicuously absent, with one or two possible exceptions (Case F). Hoards, which contain various objects more or less of one date, do not furnish any examples of the types discovered with interments; and the conclusion seems inevitable, not that any particular patterns were adopted exclusively for funeral purposes, but that the barrows in general belong to a period before bronze was in common use, metal at that time being scarce and only manufactured into articles of a comparatively small size, such as those usually found with burials. This conclusion is strikingly confirmed by the discovery of the whole effects of a family of the Bronze age in a cave called Heathery Burn, Co. Durham (Case D). The list included almost every type of the period which has been found elsewhere, and some that have been met with nowhere else, but not one example of either the plain celt or knife-dagger of the barrows. The distinction is not so marked in the case of pottery, though here too there seem to have been various forms confined to the barrows. Vessels that may well have been used for culinary or other domestic purposes have been frequently found associated with interments, and it is easy to believe that the skill required to mould and ornament the distinctive pottery of the barrows was not always or everywhere available, so that commoner vessels were substituted. All, however, were of home manufacture, local fabrics being sometimes distinguishable; and, whatever may have been the case with bronze, it is fairly certain that pottery from the barrows has no claim to be regarded as exotic, but was produced in the localities where found.

In addition to modes of burial, and distribution of bronze, the skull-forms throw some light on the affinities and characteristics of the inhabitants, whose remains are met with in our Round barrows; and the progress of discovery has only confirmed the rule enunciated by Dr. Thurnam, that long skulls are found in Long barrows, and short (rather than round) skulls are found in Round barrows. It is evident, however, that during the Round-barrow period the population was very mixed; in Yorkshire, for example, dolichocephalic and brachycephalic skeletons were found in very nearly equal proportions, while the earlier or Long barrows contained dolichocephalic subjects exclusively. The skulls here illustrated as specimens were described by Professor Rolleston in his contribution to *British Barrows*, and clearly exhibit the marked differences observable in Round-barrow skulls. The first (fig. 1) is that of a strong man past middle life, from a Round barrow at Helperthorpe, East Riding of Yorkshire. The body, which constituted the primary interment, had been laid on the left side, and in a contracted position, with the head to the north and the left hand up to the face, in front of which was part of a flint knife, while at the head was the tine of a red deer's antler. The cephalic index (or ratio of the skull's breadth to its length, the latter being represented by 100), is 71, which is well within the dolichocephalic limit of 75. The second skull illustrated (fig. 2) belonged to a man past middle life, and 5 ft. 7 in. in height. This too may have been a primary interment in a Round barrow at Cowlam in the same Riding, six miles from Helperthorpe; and the contracted or crouching skeleton lay on the left side, with the head to the south-east and the hands up to the face. With a cephalic index of 84, this subject must be classed as brachy-

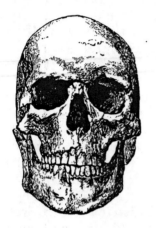

Fig. 1.—Dolichocephalic skull, Helperthorpe, E. R. Yorks.

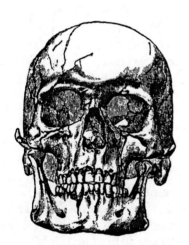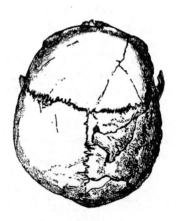

Fig. 2.—Brachycephalic skull, Cowlam, E. R. Yorks.

cephalic; the intermediate form called mesaticephalic ranging between the indices 75 and 80. It must, however, be remembered that the proportionate width of the skull is only one of many characteristics that distinguish the two types just exemplified; and the respective skeletons themselves support the view that the long and short-headed occupants of the

Round barrows belonged to different races. For instance, skeletons from the Long barrows, in which the dolichocephalic population is exclusively represented, give 5 ft. 5½ in. as the average male stature, while the brachycephalic men of the Round barrows (with index of 81–83) were on the average 5 ft. 8¼ in. in height, and stronger in proportion. The typical inhabitant of this country in the Round barrow or Bronze period has been compared by Professor Rolleston to the modern Dane; but recent excavations in the East Riding have brought to light a large proportion of intermediate skull-forms, which show an extensive fusion of races, at any rate in that part of the country.

The evidence afforded by skull-forms should be viewed in connection with the most recent pronouncements on the ethnology of early Britain from the philological point of view. According to Prof. John Rhys and Mr. Brynmor-Jones, the earliest inhabitants of these islands whose name has come down to us were the Picts; and although the question of their origin and affinities cannot be regarded as finally settled, it seems clear that the people whom Julius Caesar represents as claiming descent from the aboriginal islanders were the Picts, who eventually found a home in North Britain, and retained their language and institutions latest on the east coast of Scotland, in portions of the region between Clackmannan and Banff. One of the most remarkable facts known about the Picts is the absence among them of the institution of marriage as known to the Aryan peoples; and in later times succession is known to have been through the mother, pointing back to a time when society was based on matriarchy. The same conclusion as to the probable non-Aryan origin of the Picts is warranted also by their peculiarities of speech, but remains of their language are unfortunately scanty. It was eventually overloaded by words borrowed from the language of subsequent invaders, but a non-Aryan element is still discernible. In the sixth and fifth centuries before our era there were important movements in the Keltic world of the Continent, and branches of the race reached the Mediterranean, establishing themselves later in the country called after them Galatia, in Asia Minor. It is unlikely that these islands remained unaffected by the Keltic migrations, but it was probably long before that date that a branch of that widespread family settled in these islands. The Keltic-speaking pioneers are now generally spoken of as *Goidel* or *Gaoidheal*, the latter being the modern form of the name, which is

pronounced and spelt in English *Gael*.   In all probability they
came first from the nearest parts of the Continent, where they
had been neighbours of the true Kelts.   These in the time of
Caesar (about 50 B.C.) inhabited Gaul, which comprised ancient
France, Belgium, Switzerland, and North Italy, as well as parts
of Spain.   The Goidels had presumably occupied most of the
island south of the Firths of Clyde and Forth before another
people of Keltic speech began to make incursions on these
shores.   The new-comers are known as Brythons, and it is
from them that the name Britain is derived.   A chronological
limit for this second wave of Keltic immigration is possibly
afforded by the express mention of Britain in the record of
the voyage of Pytheas, a Greek of Marseilles who explored
north-west Europe about the time of the philosopher Aristotle,
towards the end of the fourth century B.C.; but the name may
have been merely put into his mouth by Strabo, who quotes
from a lost original.   Some time before Caesar's invasion
a third conquest of this island by people with a similar
language had taken place, and as he found the Belgae in
possession of the south, it is evident that by that time the
Brythons, who had been steadily driving their predecessors,
the Goidels, to the extremities of Britain and probably into
Ireland, were themselves being pressed northward by more
recent invaders who have left their name to Belgium.

The Brythonic and Goidelic divisions of the Keltic Aryans
(in the linguistic sense of the terms) have been conveniently
distinguished by philologists as P and Q Kelts respectively,
with reference to one of several marked contrasts in their
languages.   In the Goidelic group of dialects, embracing at
the present day the Gaelic of Ireland, of the Isle of Man, and
of Scotland, *qu* corresponds to *p* in the Brythonic of Wales,
Brittany, and (till recently) Cornwall; and a similar distinction
is observed in the Latin and Umbro-Samnite dialects of ancient
Italy: thus the name Pontius is a dialect variety of the
Roman Quintius; and the Welsh *map* (now *mab*), a boy or son,
corresponds to the Gaelic *mac* or *maq*.   It is fairly certain that
the non-Aryan aborigines are largely represented in the present
population of this country; and it appears from their language
that the Goidels coalesced with them to a large extent,
especially when Goidel and Pict were confronted by their
common enemy, the Brython.   Indeed, the term Goidelic
should strictly be confined to the mixed population of Aryan
and non-Aryan language in possession of the country when
the Brythons arrived.

Another difficulty is to associate the introduction of metal-working with any of the waves of invasion already noticed. It has been pointed out by Sir John Lubbock (now Lord Avebury) that what is recorded of the Phoenicians in the Mediterranean affords a clue to the earliest date of metal-working in this country. Strabo (B.C. 54–A.D. 24) expressly says that in early times the Phoenicians carried on the tin trade from Cadiz, and this port was perhaps founded by them partly for the trade with Cornwall, to which it was nearer than to Tyre or Sidon. Sir John Evans concurs in the view that between B.C. 1500 and B.C. 1200 the Phoenicians were already acquainted with the mineral fields of Britain, bronze having been known in Egypt long before that date; and he adds that the use of tin, and probably also of copper, would date back in Britain to a still earlier epoch. The Phoenicians, or those who traded with them, would not land in Britain and discover tin spontaneously; it must have been a knowledge that the inhabitants of Britain were already producers of this valuable metal that originated the commerce.

That tin or copper was worked here before 2000 B.C. is however very improbable, though one school of archaeologists in Scandinavia, while allowing that metal was known earlier in this country than in their own, place the beginning of their Bronze age about 1800 B.C., and the use of copper still earlier, in the neolithic period. Another view is that bronze was introduced about five centuries later, the Bronze age in Scandinavia lasting from about the twelfth to the fourth century B.C. For the beginning of bronze in Great Britain and Ireland the date suggested by Sir John Evans lies between the two above mentioned, and is more likely to be too late than too early; if B.C. 1800 is a possible date for Sweden and Denmark, it is a probable one for our islands.

Sir John Evans has provisionally divided our Bronze age into three parts:—(1) the period of the Barrows, characterized by primitive forms hardly found apart from burials; (2) the period of the flanged celt and the tanged spear-head, represented by the Arreton Down find; and (3) the period of the bronze hoards, when swords and socketed celts and spear-heads are most conspicuous. To this last period he would assign four or five centuries, and an approximate date is thus reached for the close of the Barrow period, about 900 B.C. This date must be compared with that reached on other grounds by various archaeologists. Dr. Sophus Müller of Copenhagen is of opinion that cremation was not practised long before the year

1000 B.C., though it appeared earlier in the south of Europe than in the north, and was characteristic of the Aryan peoples. On both points Professor Ridgeway of Cambridge agrees with him, and an interval of a century or two is thus provided for the interments that show contemporary burials by both cremation and inhumation. The former method is known to have lasted down to the end of the Late Keltic period and into Roman times, while it helps to explain why burials of the later Bronze period are unproductive of metallic objects. It may have been a change of belief as to the spirit-world or economy of the still precious metal that resulted in the abolition of all furniture from Bronze age graves later than the Barrow period; and the large number of cinerary urns discovered and preserved possibly represent the period during which swords and spear-heads of bronze were manu-factured and carried by our population.

The elements of that population have already been indi-cated, but something must be said as to the immediate source of the Bronze culture in these islands. In the description of the Cases, forms will be noticed which appear to belong for the most part to certain definite localities abroad, and though such finds are rare in Britain, they throw some light on our early connections with the Continent. Thus, a remarkable dagger (fig. 48) from the Thames was either imported from Italy during the *terramara* period or copied later from such a specimen at some point on the trade-routes between the Channel and Italy. Again, the halberts of Ireland are very like those of Spain, which can be approximately dated, while specimens are also found in Italy and North Germany. On other grounds it seems likely that while Ireland derived its earliest bronze or copper forms from the Mediterranean by way of Spain, Britain in the Bronze period was more closely connected with the north of France, which was in its turn supplied to a certain extent from Italy through the passes of the Alps and by sea to Marseilles. A map prepared by the Hon. John Abercromby shows that the 'drinking-cup,' the earliest well-defined type of Barrow pottery in this country, occurs uniformly on the east coasts of Scotland and North England, though there are clusters also in Derbyshire and Wilts.; and it may be inferred that these vessels were introduced from Scandinavia or the Netherlands by a people scarcely acquainted with metals. Whether these new-comers can be identified with any race of which we find linguistic traces cannot be affirmed, but that they arrived before the

Aryans seems the most probable hypothesis. The Aryans who are credited with the introduction of cremation into Europe are now thought to have found the art of metal-working already established in certain parts, and to have actually retarded civilisation in the districts they appropriated. Such a view would suit the conditions in our islands very well; and if 1000 B.C. be taken as a central date for the earliest cremation urns in the barrows, we may assign the 'drinking-cups' and those 'food-vessels' found with unburnt burials, and frequently with bronze objects, to the pre-Aryan population, in part descended from our remoter neolithic ancestors.

As in the foregoing pages mention has been made of a chronological system in connection with prehistoric objects, it may be well to explain in a few words the method by which it has been possible to establish anything like absolute dates for the antiquities of the Bronze age—a method which is principally associated with the name of Professor Oscar Montelius, of Stockholm.

The attempt to assign absolute dates to objects earlier than any historical records is based upon the previous establishment of a *relative* chronology obtained through a classification by sequence of types. It is found that the bronze antiquities of almost any country can be divided into a number of consecutive series in which the development of types of different objects, especially axe-heads and brooches, can be clearly traced. It is further found that the characteristic types of one series are hardly ever associated with those of another, and that the only objects which overlap are those of the end of one series and the beginning of the next: a type of the earliest series, for example, will never be found in the same tomb or deposit with one of the third, or a type of the second with one of the fourth. From this it may be safely inferred that the period covered by each series must have lasted long enough to completely displace the types of that which preceded it, and its duration is therefore assumed to have been not less than about a century and a half, though it may have been longer.

Sometimes, however, the date of a later series can be exactly determined, because the objects which compose it occur with types also found in Central Europe and Italy, and these in their turn come into relation with the old historical civilisation of which the dates are known. For example, a certain form of hammered bronze vessel found in Etruscan tombs at Bologna also occurs in Brandenburg, Saxony, Denmark, and Sweden, in every case with objects belonging to a period to which the dates 700–600 B.C. can reasonably be assigned. Objects of this kind give a date to their group and supply a fixed point from which that of the earlier series can be approximately defined: by such means the beginning of the Bronze age in Northern Europe has been carried back to about 1800 B.C. The weak point of the method is that though the dates of the later divisions may be regarded as certain, those of the earlier become more and more vague as the remotest period is approached; for the objects which can be brought into relation with the early civilisations diminish in number as the scale is ascended: the higher limit is therefore not a fixed but a wavering line, which may have to be constantly redrawn in the light of increasing knowledge. Some periods, too, must have been longer than others, and it is very hard to say what their average length should be. But in spite of these inevitable drawbacks the system may be relied on within a few centuries even for the higher limit, while it yields exact results for the lower: a greater precision than this we can scarcely expect to achieve. To possess anything in the nature of a date to fall back upon in the study of prehistoric antiquities is a distinct aid to the memory, and even the most provisional of methods may be of great temporary use to the student, provided he never forgets that it is constantly liable to revision. Opportunities for giving an absolute date to prehistoric objects of the Bronze age within the Mediterranean area are more frequent than in the case of those from the north of the Alps, because inscribed Egyptian scarabs belonging to particular dynasties are occasionally found with them, or because they themselves occur in Egyptian tombs of known antiquity. Certain phases of the Aegean Bronze-age culture known as the Mycenaean, and the earlier stage which preceded it, have been dated in this way. Scarabs of Amenhetep III and Thii (about 1450) have been found at Mycenae and Ialysos; scarabs of 2000–2500 B.C. have occurred among pre-Mycenaean remains at Hagios Onuphrios in Crete, while Mycenaean and pre-Mycenaean pottery has been excavated from various Egyptian sites dating from near the beginning of the first millennium B.C. back to the period of the twelfth dynasty at Kahun (B.C. 2500–2300). From facts like these, clues are obtained which are of great assistance in the difficult task of bringing prehistory and history into relation with each other, and co-ordinating our knowledge of contemporaneous but dissimilar cultures in very early times.

DESCRIPTION OF CASES.

Cases 1, 2.

In the upper part are shown some of the larger flat celts from various sites in Ireland, smaller specimens being arranged to the left of the main shelf. Though the exact localities are in most cases unknown, specimens of this kind have been found in most of the Irish counties, and are generally of copper, practically pure. In twelve analyses published by Mr. Geo. Coffey the copper is seen to vary from 96·46 to 99·44 per cent. of the whole, while tin and antimony combined range between a mere trace and 1·09 per cent. In the majority of cases the tin did not exceed 0·51 per cent., while seven of the twelve specimens contained no more than 0·1 per cent. of that metal (Case D). In such circumstances it is admissible to call these *copper* celts rather than bronze; and it is evident from their shapes that they immediately succeed, and are derived from, the stone celts of the neolithic period. The broadened cutting edge is essentially a metallic form, due to hammering; but the connection with examples in stone is further illustrated by a curious reaction on the stone celt, some specimens of which display a broadened edge copied from the metallic celt in use during the transition period from stone to metal. The probable development of the celt from the neolithic form to the types in use at the opening of the Iron age is shown in the description of Case 11 by examples taken from the collection (p. 40).

The earliest type, common in Ireland, is relatively broad, rounded at both ends; then appeared a square butt (fig. 16, *a*), which gradually became thinner and was sometimes rounded off, while the sides became straighter, giving a more slender appearance to the celt (fig. 16, *b*). Flanges formed by beating up the edges are only seen in rudimentary form in the copper celts, while stop-ridges and ornament are altogether wanting in that metal. Examples of the more developed forms are arranged in the lower part of the Case. The pins here shown are all of the last period of the Bronze age, and are all represented in Danish finds. The cup-shaped head may be compared with the terminals of gold bracelets from Ireland (fig. 138), and the large pin engraved with characteristic ornament is an exaggerated example of a common type, with the circular head bent over (fig. 3). The implement here illustrated (fig. 4) is probably a flesh-hook, used ceremonially like that of the priests in Eli's time, and is the second found in Irish

bogs. The middle section resembles several pieces, with simple rings in place of the birds, from France (Case E) and the Swiss lake-dwellings, and a hooked portion, evidently from an implement of the same kind, has been found in a hoard of bronze near Norwich.

Heavy rings with transverse perforations (fig. 5) are common in Ireland, and are with reason supposed to have formed, with pins passed through the holes, brooches to fasten the dress in the same way as the penannular brooches of the same country in the Viking period.

The remarkable series of bronzes here exhibited from the townland of Dowris, King's County, formed part of a hoard found about the year 1825 in a part of Whigsborough, called Derreens. Though now boggy, the soil was at that time under cultivation, and was no doubt covered with copse and underwood when the deposit was made, probably by a bronze-founder who worked on the spot. At least a horse-load of these gold-coloured relics were found together, some pieces in excellent condition, others broken up to be remelted, though a few were damaged by the finders

FIG. 3.—Pin with ornamented head, Ireland. ¼

themselves. The rubbers of sandstone and the rough cake of metal point to the local manufacture of these articles, and most are of types commonly found in Ireland. The trumpets (plate II, 4, 8, and Cases 3, 4) are of three varieties, the curved specimens having the mouthpiece at the end or at one side, and the straight

FIG. 4.—Flesh-hook, Dunaverney bog, Co. Antrim. ⅛

cylinders forming parts of larger instruments. The horns were cast in one piece, the spikes being, perhaps, survivals of original rivet-heads. Of the so-called bells (plate II, 2), some are pear-shaped, while others are almost spherical, all containing loose clappers of metal or stone, but so constructed that little or no

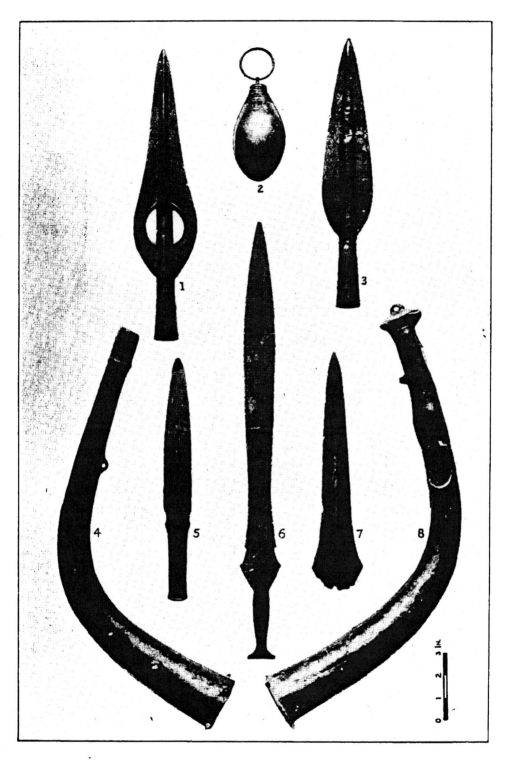

PLATE II. PART OF HOARD, DOWRIS, KING'S Co.
(Cases 1, 2, *see* p. 28.)

sound can be obtained from them. Socketed knives and spear-heads are also included in the find, as well as a curious hammer-head (fig. 6); and many of the objects were contained in a bronze cauldron of 21 in. diameter, formed of thin plates riveted together, similar to that exhibited in the lower part of Case 14. The golden tint of many of the specimens may be due to the peaty nature of the soil, but very closely resembles the condition of some bronze implements found in the Thames (Case A). The composition of the metal varies, but all the pieces have a con-siderable proportion of tin, unlike the common flat celt of Ireland. One of the Dowris celts contains 85·23 per cent. of copper, 13·11

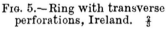

Fig. 5.—Ring with transverse perforations, Ireland. ⅔

Fig. 6.—Hammer, Dowris, King's Co.

of tin, 1·14 of lead, and traces of sulphur and carbon, while the waste metal yielded on analysis 89 per cent. of copper, 11 of tin, and a mere trace of lead, iron, and silver.

Cases 3, 4.

In the lower part of Case 4 are three bronze vessels belonging to the Dowris hoard in Cases 1, 2. The largest is in the form of a cinerary urn, of a type rarely found in Northern Europe, and evidently derived from Italy. Isolated examples of these Etruscan products have occurred in Brittany, England, and Ireland, as well as in Denmark and North Germany; and their spread was undoubtedly due to the active intercourse with the South brought about by the amber trade, which can be traced back for many centuries before Christ, while the abundance of gold in Ireland would also draw merchants to the West at an early date.

Vessels of this conical form (plate iv, 2) with ornamental handles have been ascribed on sufficient grounds to about 500 B.C., and may be assumed to be of this date wherever they are found. The two smaller vessels are less determinate, and have angular clamps to strengthen the base, similar to, but larger than, those on the largest vessel, which is much mended by patching, rivets and not solder being used for the purpose. All the bronze vessels of this period seem to have been of very thin metal, and large specimens are exhibited in Case 14. They were not well adapted for cooking purposes; and some special function, perhaps of a ceremonial kind, must be assigned to those with an incurved reeded lip to which are attached a pair of ring-handles (plate iv, 1). Several have been found in Ireland and Scotland, but they are unknown outside the British Isles.

The trumpet was probably connected with warfare, and is especially common in Ireland, where two distinct kinds are found—those cast in one piece, and those formed of sheet-metal turned over and riveted to form the tube. In some the mouthpiece is at the end (plate ii, 4), in others at the side (plate ii, 8), like those made of elephant tusks in Central Africa. Those from the Dowris hoard already noticed (p. 28) illustrate the loops for hanging and the spikes near the mouth of the implement, while the straight lengths belonged to larger instruments, like one found at Caprington, Ayrshire. The Kelts of the second century B.C. are known to have used a large number of trumpets in war; but, though there is little evidence of date, the Irish examples probably belong, like the *lurer* or twisted horns of Denmark, to the close of the Bronze period. The objects found at Dowris serve to date the type illustrated, but it is probable that the riveted examples belong to the Iron age. In England trumpets have been found in the Witham at Tattershall, and at Battle, Sussex, the former having the edges united by soldering (a process unknown in the Bronze period), and closely resembling one found in Hanover.

Bucklers of embossed bronze have been found in England and Wales, Scotland and Ireland, not always singly, but never with other objects that afforded definite information as to their date. Being of embossed metal, they must have demanded considerable skill on the part of the manufacturer, and are generally assigned to a late stage in our Bronze age. Two from Wales, constituting a pair, are shown, and the arrangement of the handle is seen at the back, while the small moveable tongues of bronze may have served to attach a strap for carrying the shield. Both are from peat-bogs, one near Aberystwyth, Cardiganshire (plate i, 2), and the other at Moel Siabod, near Capel Curig, Carnarvonshire. The smaller example, ornamented with large bosses, is from Athenry, Co. Galway, and may have formed the centre of a larger shield of leather or wood, in this way resembling the Roman bosses exhibited in the Central Saloon, Case D. It was, however, more probably used as a buckler, to parry a blow, and not attached to the arm by means of straps. Three distinct sizes are observable in examples from the British Isles, with diameters of nearly 24 in., of 12 to 18 in., and about 9 in. respectively, and all are provided with a central boss to protect the hand. One found at Harlech, Merionethshire, has concentric rings without the embossed knobs, and closely resembles one from Bingen, Rhenish Hesse; but examples in Scandinavia not only differ in details from our types, but were mostly imported from Etruria, where several have been found. A buckler found on the island of Falster, however, may have come from Britain, and one of the numerous rock-carvings (fig. 7) on the east coast of the Skager Rak represents a warrior bearing in his left hand a shield which may have

FIG. 7.—Rock-carving, Nedre Hede, Quille, Bohuslän.

been copied from a British original. This is only one of several indications of intercourse between Scandinavia and the British Isles, another being the presence of Irish celts in Sweden and Denmark. If the scale can be relied on, the shield in the Swedish rock-carving corresponds in dimensions with that illustrated from Wales (plate 1, 2), $26\frac{1}{2}$ in. in diameter; though the ornamentation is more perfectly reproduced in the smaller buckler from the Isis. It will be noticed that the large and small bosses occur on separate examples from the Thames (Cases 6, 7), the former being probably the earlier type; and both here shown have evidently been damaged by spear and sword thrusts. The commonest British form is that with many bands of small bosses separated by raised concentric rings (plate 1, 2), and it should be added that all were no doubt produced from a thicker disc of metal by hammering, there being no indication that the metal was cast in its present form.

Case 5

A cinerary urn (fig. 8), sometimes associated with Bronwen the Fair, was found in 1813, containing the burnt bones of a woman. On one fragment was noticed a slight green stain as of bronze, but the form and quality of the urn are unusual, and in the absence of other evidence it can only be tentatively assigned to the later Bronze age. It was inverted in a cist of flag-stones within a cairn about twelve paces from the River Alaw, in what is known as the 'islet of Bronwen' (Ynys Bronwen), Anglesey. It was at or near this spot that the aunt of Caractacus is said to have been buried about 50 A.D., but the cinerary urn is probably earlier by some centuries, and was itself interred in an older grave, to which some unburnt bones and fragments of a 'drinking-cup' found at the same time no doubt belonged.

Other sepulchral pottery from the district also shows certain peculiarities of texture and decoration. On the shore of Porth Dafarch, a small harbour in Holyhead Island, was a mound 30 ft. in diameter which had been lowered by ploughing, the stones that formed a cairn being scattered about. Under a large flat stone was a cinerary urn containing the smaller urn with herring-bone decoration. The former measured 13 in. at the mouth and was ornamented within the lip, but only the fragment here exhibited was preserved. A second interment was close by, of a similar character: a larger urn containing among the ashes the smaller one with incurved lip. It is suggested that these contained the remains of a mother and daughter, but a very small bronze rivet, found in the sand, gave little information as to the period.

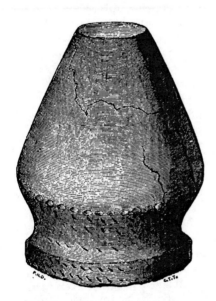

Fig. 8.—Cinerary urn, Ynys Bronwen, Anglesey. ⅕

In many parts of Anglesey, but especially near Holyhead, are to be seen groups of low mounds on rough, uncultivated ground, which on examination prove to contain circular walls of stone, partly demolished and overgrown with turf, gorse, or bracken. The space enclosed by these walls is generally from 15 to 20 ft. in diameter, with the opening always facing the south-east, and having two large upright stones about 4 or 5 ft. high as door-posts. These sites of human habitations are usually in clusters of five or more, but at Ty Mawr on Holyhead mountain form a village of more than fifty huts. Such settlements are usually situated so as to be sheltered by rising ground from the north-west winds, and are generally protected from hostile attack by rude walls of dry masonry or by precipitous rocks. From time immemorial they have been known as Cyttiau'r Gwyddelod (huts of Irishmen or Aborigines), and may have been originally roofed by converging stones laid horizontally, forming bee-hive huts such as occur in Ireland and elsewhere; but it is more probable that the roof consisted of turf supported on horizontal poles. Though the absence of metal in many cases affords a presumption that these dwellings belong to the Stone age, bronze implements have certainly been found on more than one occasion as well as a mould for casting them; and traces of occupation in Roman times are abundant and unmistakable. A discovery of Late Keltic remains has recently been made on the site of 'Irishmen's huts' at Treceiri, on one of the peaks of Yr Eifl, Carnarvonshire.

Of the hut-circles two kinds have been excavated in Anglesey, chiefly by the Hon. W. O. Stanley. In 1862 a typical mound at Ty Mawr contained what seems to have been simply a dwelling-place, the illustration (fig. 9) showing the enclosed area divided into compartments by upright stones; and against the partitions

Fig. 9.—View of hut-circle, Ty Mawr, Holyhead.

as well as the inner wall of the hut, were upright slabs forming what are considered to have been fireplaces. The circles contained flat and round stones, all bearing traces of fire, the former perhaps used for baking food, the latter for boiling water in skins or other receptacles. Implements of gritstone for grinding corn were also found, as well as remains of shell-fish in a heap. The ground-plan (fig. 10) shows the arrangement of another type of buildings, perhaps used as workshops for smelting and working metals. The fireplaces were constructed of large stones, generally in the centre of the hut, with small fireplaces flanking the central one or arranged round the wall of the building, in some instances with a well-formed chimney in the thickness of the hut-wall. The rude stone pounders or mullers, the mortars or basins and heavy flat stones set in the floor for grinding or breaking stone or some hard material, presented no appearance of having been used for preparing food. Broken quartz from the copper lode in the neighbourhood, slag and clay-lined fireplaces, point to the smelting of copper and iron ore; and in this connection may be

D

mentioned the bronze implements (Case A) found together under a stone in one of the Ty Mawr huts, as well as a mould for casting spear-heads and celts of the same form, found in Anglesey. Whereas in the rude dwellings the saddle-back querns and mullers were of gritstone, the grinding and pounding-stones found in the supposed workshops are of hard trap, well adapted for crushing the ores of the district.

More advanced domestic implements are found at Pen-y-Bonc

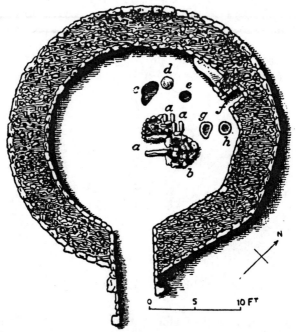

Fig. 10.—Plan of workshop, Ty Mawr, Holyhead. *a*, fire-place ; *b*, platform ; *c*, hole containing sharpening-stones; *d*, pounding-stone; *e*, hole; *f*, fireplace and chimney ; *g*, rubbing-stone ; *h*, mortar.

in connection with Roman coins of the first and second centuries, as well as 'Samian' ware and cinerary urns of Roman origin. The quern or hand-mill is generally held to have been introduced about the Christian era, and Agricola is known to have conquered and settled Anglesey about A. D. 78 ; but though these remains, like a carnelian intaglio found at Porth Dafarch, are undeniably connected with Roman civilisation, there can be no doubt as to the much earlier date of many of the structures.

Cases 6, 7.

Below is a series of stone antiquities from several brochs excavated by Sir Francis Tress Barry near Keiss, on the coast of

Caithness. No precise date has yet been assigned to these strue-tures, but they were evidently occupied for defensive purposes at

FIG 11.—Dun Telve broch, Glenelg, Inverness-shire.

different periods and gradually filled up, so that objects of widely different dates may be sometimes found together in the ruins.

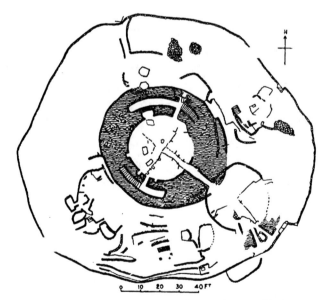

FIG. 12.—Ground-plan of Road broch, Keiss, Caithness.

The most distinctive among these are no doubt of ' Late Keltic ' origin, and fragments of Samian ware point unmistakably to con-tact with Roman civilisation; but, on the other hand, a number of painted pebbles have been found in three of the Keiss brochs, remarkably like those from Mas d'Azil, in the Pyrenees, which date from the transition between the palaeolithic and neolithic periods.   The excavations are published by Dr. Joseph Anderson, of Edinburgh, who describes the typical broch as a huge dry-built circular tower, rising on a base of about 60 ft. in diameter to a

Fig. 13.—Road broch, Keiss, Caithness (from within).

height of about 50 ft., like that at Mousa, Shetland.   In its elevation the tower was a hollow cylinder, the thickness of wall being from 12 to 15 ft., round a court of about 30 ft. in diameter open to the sky.   As all the windows looked into the interior court, there was no opening on the outside except the tunnel-like doorway about 5 yds. long leading into the court, the actual door being a slab of stone strengthened by a drawbar resting in holes made for it in the walls.   There was usually a guard-chamber behind the door and at the foot of the stairs leading to upper galleries, while the chambers on the ground floor were reached by separate doors. The galleries and staircases were constructed in the thickness of the wall, and the Dun Telve broch (fig. 11), which is still 30 ft. high, has five such galleries one above the other. The typical ground-plan (fig. 12) recalls that of the hut-circles of Wales and Cornwall, while the vertical slabs of stone in the enclosed area (fig. 13) are again seen at Ty Mawr (fig. 9). The number and distribution of the brochs still testify to their former importance, the round grass-covered mounds which now conceal their ruins being thickly scattered over the best arable lands near the coast and for long distances up the river valleys. They are confined to Scotland and most numerous in the northern counties, over eighty having been counted in Caithness, sixty in Sutherland, seventy in Orkney, and seventy-five in Shetland, while only seven are known in the south of Scotland.

The bucklers in the upper part of this Case have been already referred to (p. 31). The chapes or scabbard-tips also shown from

Fig. 14.—Chape of sword-scabbard, Thames at Amerden, Bucks. ⅓

the Thames belonged to leaf-shaped swords and not to daggers, to which their actual length rather corresponds. The greater part of the blade was protected by wood or leather, which passed inside the chape and was affixed to it by means of rivets, while the point of the weapon in no case seems to have reached the end of the sheath. Wooden scabbards without metal chapes found in Denmark are also considerably longer than the blade. The metal chapes are cast in one piece, and the uniform thinness of the metal points to great skill in casting. Most have a curved outline (fig. 14), but one found with the buckler above in the Isis, near Dorchester, Oxon., has straight tapering sides, while the winged or boat-shaped specimen (fig. 15) is of another type, which eventually assumed extraordinary proportions in France (Case N), and has been found on the end of an iron sword. Simpler forms of the winged type occur in England and Ireland; and the tapering pattern, which is seen to be frequently found in the Thames, is also known from Scotland, smaller examples occurring in the north of France, but being no doubt derived from the English type.

Cases 8–10.

Deposits of bronze in the soil or other hiding-place are generally known as 'hoards,' and have been divided into three main classes, viz:—(1) Personal hoards: personal property buried for temporary concealment, but never recovered by the original owner.   (2) Merchants' hoards: a stock of implements or weapons ready for use and probably carried from place to place by travelling dealers or by the manufacturers themselves.   (3) Founders' hoards: broken or disused implements and weapons collected and packed together by travelling tinkers for remelting, as is shown by the frequent occurrence, in this class, of moulds for the manufacture of celts, spear-heads, and other forms.

Hoards are of special importance as showing within certain limits what objects were contemporary, and Sir John Evans draws

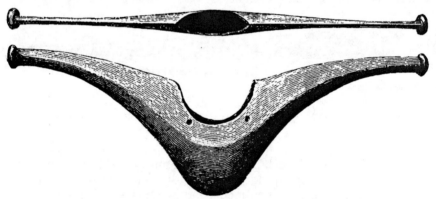

Fig. 15.—Chape of sword-scabbard, Thames. $\frac{1}{2}$

several conclusions from the study of those found in this country. The chief points are :—

1. That flat celts and knife-daggers such as are known from British barrows occur very rarely in hoards.

2. Flanged celts and palstaves are occasionally found together, but palstaves are often found with socketed celts.

3. Tanged implements of any sort are rarely found with socketed specimens.

4. Torcs or twisted collars are more often associated with palstaves than with socketed celts, and are mainly confined to our western counties.

5. Metal moulds and rough lumps of copper are generally associated with socketed celts.

It may be argued from the above that the hoards are as a class later than the period of the barrows, and that the socket was recognised universally as an improvement on the tang for the attachment of the handle, though the palstave, which was derived from the French winged celt (p. 41) and is found with the Gaulish torc, was a final form and remained in use as long as the socketed celt. Finally, the use of metal for moulds in place of clay was not possible till the last stage of the Bronze period.

Special attention may be drawn to a series of spear-heads, rings, and fragments of swords from Hampshire which owe their peculiar colour to burial in peat. They probably form part of the hoard found at Hogmoor in 1870 and described in an appendix to the *Natural History of Sclborne*, a peculiar feature being the hacked edges of many of the pieces. The spear-heads are of graceful form and excellent workmanship ; and a chape, similar to but smaller than those in the preceding Case, still contains the tip of a sword. The hoard from Shoebury, Essex, contains two pieces common in Switzerland but practically unknown here : an engraved bracelet, like a gold specimen from Tisbury (fig. 141), and a winged celt of peculiar form, like fig. 130 (right). A socketed chisel, like one from the Thames (Case A) and the Swiss lake-dwellings (fig. 133), appears in the hoard from Meldreth, Cambs., which also contains part of a cauldron like one in Case 14 (plate IV, 1), though smaller. Knives of hog-back type with a perforation occur at Meldreth ; Bromley-by-Bow, Essex ; Hoo, Kent ; and Minster, Thanet (plate III). The last locality furnished some peculiar hollow loops, the use of which is not yet ascertained (plate III and hoard from Broadward, Shropshire) ; also a socketed knife (cf. Bromley, Hoo, and Dowris hoards) and part of a sickle (as fig. 67, Taplow). The exceptional spearheads in the Broadward hoard resemble one from Plaistow (fig. 78), and are noticed under Case D (p. 85). The hoard from Stibbard, Norfolk, contains palstaves fresh from the mould and untrimmed ; and jets, or waste pieces of cast metal, from the mouths of moulds for socketed celts occur at Kensington, London, and with part of a bronze mould at Rochester, Kent. A jet from a mould with three instead of two runners is in Case B. The socketed gouges which are of frequent occurrence in the hoards may have been used to extract the burnt clay core from socketed celts after casting.

In the lower part of Cases 8, 9 are arranged, according to counties, celts of ordinary kinds found in Britain, the more remarkable specimens being exhibited in Case D.

Case 11.

A series of celts is here shown to illustrate the apparent development of that implement from the beginning of the Bronze period. They have all been found in the British Isles, and may be regarded as representative for that area. In tracing the various stages through which the implement seems to have passed, we can only incidentally mention forms which occur in other countries, where the development took other directions; but foreign examples may be studied under their respective countries

FIG. 16.—STAGES IN EVOLUTION OF THE CELT.

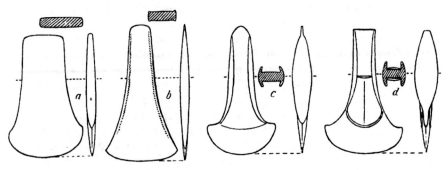

From stone to metallic form.

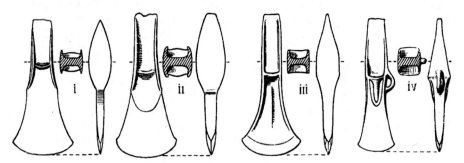

Growth of the stop-ridge.

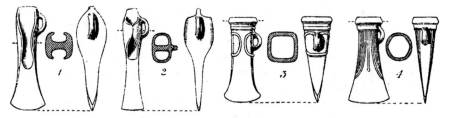

Growth of the wings.

below. The earliest celts are evidently metal copies of the commonest stone implement of the neolithic period, and have convex faces and sides, which are perhaps best illustrated by the Butterwick example (fig. 33), but may be represented here by fig. 16, *a.* It was subsequently found that the same purpose could be served by reducing the width of the celt, and the hammering necessary

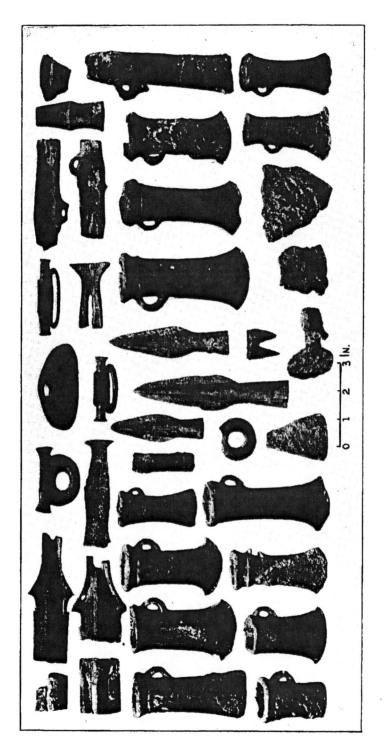

PLATE III. HOARD OF BRONZE, MINSTER, THANET.

(Case 10 *see* p. 39.)

to harden the edge resulted in an expansion of this part of the implement (b). The form of haft in use at that time no doubt resembled that of the neolithic period found in Solway Moss and exhibited in Case B ; but it was found in practice that the axe-head could be fixed more firmly in a cleft stick (fig. 54) by beating up the edges into flanges (c), and by providing a rise or angle about halfway down each face to prevent the head splitting the handle when in use. These improvements are seen on the flanged celt with slight stop-ridge (d), and were in some cases gradually accentuated, till the flanges become shorter (i, ii) and the stop-ridge is amalgamated with them (iii). Meanwhile that part of the celt covered by the prongs of the handle was made thinner to economise the metal, and comparatively deep grooves were thus provided for the reception of the handle, which was at first secured by binding and later by the addition of a loop, through which a cord passed behind the angle of the haft (Case B). This form is generally known as the palstave (iii, iv), an Icelandic word which in modern times denotes a narrow spade or spud used in agriculture.

As the hoards show, this form of celt was in use down to the end of the Bronze age, but there was a contemporary form derived ultimately from the same original, though by different stages. The socketed celt, perhaps the commonest form in these islands, was in all probability due to a continental development of the flanges at the expense of the stop-ridge. Thus in No. 1 the prongs of the handle would be held firmly enough by the arched wings that nearly meet midway between the butt and cutting edge. What is apparently a later form (2) has the wings nearer the butt and a loop added at the side for further security. With the increase of the wings a central partition or septum was no longer necessary, and disappeared when the socketed celt was rendered possible by the introduction of core-casting. The transition is marked by specimens (3) which are ornamented with crescents recalling the outline of the wings; and the later forms (3, 4), with the opening square or angular instead of oval, are merely local varieties, found more often in England than in Ireland.

Cases 12–20.

The pottery exhibited in these Cases as well as below Cases B, D, F, may be regarded as sepulchral, not only in the sense that most, if not all, of it was recovered from human interments, but also because it was in all probability manufactured expressly for funeral purposes and not for domestic use (p. 57). In many cases nothing is known of the circumstances in which these vessels were discovered, but it may be assumed that the majority had been deposited with the dead in 'barrows' (Anglo-Saxon *beorh, bearw* = mount, hill).

The use of this term is preferable to that of the Latin *tumulus*, which means a mound of any kind, not necessarily sepulchral, but there are other terms still in use locally, such as Low (Anglo-Saxon *hlaewe* = hill, mound) in Derbyshire and Staffordshire, and Howe (Danish) in Yorkshire, to denote these grave-mounds. They are generally of earth, though on the downs chalk is very often used for the purpose, and in other districts stones of various sizes, in which case the word 'cairn' is more appropriate. In size and shape many differences have been observed, even in the same district, but they may be roughly classed as Long and Round barrows; and while such enormous structures as Silbury Hill in Wiltshire must be regarded as exceptions, it should be borne in mind that many existing barrows that are scarcely noticeable may have been originally of more imposing proportions and been specially exposed to denudation. For reasons that have already been noticed (p. 16), the Long barrows may here be left out of account, as definitely belonging to the neolithic period, but a few general remarks may be added with regard to Round barrows in this country. It is usual to speak of them and the pottery they contained as British, but though the name is correct in the sense that this collection is from barrows in the British Isles, it is anything but certain that the country was already in the hands of Britons when the first Round barrows were raised (p. 22).

As a rule the Bronze age barrows are circular, with a diameter of 50-100 ft., and a present height of 2-6 ft., forming in section the outline of a cone or an inverted bowl (figs. 27, 28). In some cases they were surrounded by a ditch or ring of detached standing stones, which are, however, sometimes covered by the material of the mound; and it has been often observed that the circle of the stones or ditch is incomplete, a feature that occurs also on cup-marked stones (below Case C) of the period, and may have had a ceremonial significance. The disc-shaped barrows of Wiltshire, however, have a complete ring formed by a ditch within a bank; and in the central area one or more diminutive mounds mark the interments on the level area within. According to the late Dr. Thurnam, burials in this last class of barrows were almost exclusively after cremation, but not in cinerary urns, the ashes being deposited in small cavities scooped out of the chalk rock.

The barrows are found in groups, and also in isolation, but are irregularly placed, and as a rule have no apparent connection with each other. They are most conspicuous on the open chalk downs of Wiltshire, Dorset, and the East Riding of Yorkshire, but are also common in Derbyshire, and may once have been more numerous than at present in other districts which have been under cultivation for centuries; but the distribution of the earliest type of sepulchral pottery shows that the population which raised the earliest barrows was concentrated on the east coast of Scotland, and in the English districts specified.

Scattered throughout the material of the mound are constantly found animal bones, which have been generally broken to extract the marrow, also chippings and waste pieces of flint as well as potsherds. These last are not as a rule of the same ware as the sepulchral vases presently to be noticed, but apparently belonged to domestic vessels ; and it is remarkable that the fragments do not belong together but to several different vessels, so that they cannot be regarded as remnants of the pottery used at the funeral feast and subsequently shattered over the grave.

Though many barrows retain no trace of an interment, the majority were no doubt used on more than one occasion, and enclosed the remains of men, women, and children ; but instances are known of the erection of an extensive barrow over the solitary body of an infant. The method of deposit varied at different periods, and in spite of the fact that both practices were for some time contemporaneous, it may be laid down as a general rule that burial of the dead in a contracted position was in vogue before cremation and the deposit of the ashes in pottery urns. Coffins formed of tree-trunks split and hollowed have been occasionally found in this country, and in Denmark belong to the earliest period of the Bronze age. In that country they contain the skeleton wrapped in a woollen textile, and similar remains were found at Rylston, West Riding of Yorkshire. The archaeological significance of funeral customs has already been touched on (p. 25), and it will here suffice to notice that while the unburnt burials in Round barrows are sometimes ambiguous, cremation and urn-deposit are characteristic of the Bronze age in this country.

Reserving the relative position and possible connection of interments in Round barrows for special treatment under Cases 21–30, we pass to a classification of the sepulchral pottery produced in these islands between the close of the neolithic period and the introduction of iron. All was made without the potter's wheel, and the baking was often imperfect, owing to the use of an open fire ; but the mistake of calling any of it 'sun-baked' is as common as it is elementary. The clay is generally mixed with minute pebbles, or fragments of broken flint, quartz, chalk, or shells, perhaps added intentionally to strengthen the ware : while for some of the finer vessels the clay was tempered by the admixture of grit or sharp sand. Cinerary urns may in many cases have been baked in the embers of the funeral pile.

1. *Drinking-cups* (plate v, 1–3). The name is based on Sir Richard Colt Hoare's assumption that the tall cylindrical vessels of good thin ware found almost exclusively with unburnt interments, were intended to hold liquid, either for refreshment during

the journey to the next world or to propitiate the spirit of the dead in the interests of the living.   As their precise use has yet to be explained, it is desirable to retain a term that has been so long current, though 'beaker' would in some ways be more appropriate.   As vessels of this and the following types were not placed in the grave empty, and remains of a more or less solid nature have been traced in both, it is probable that the 'drinking-cup' fulfilled the same purpose as the 'food-vessel' which succeeded it, and has been found with separate interments in the same barrow. The earlier kind is, however, practically confined to certain parts of Britain, and the only specimens that can with certainty be referred to Ireland were found in one grave at Moytirra, Co. Sligo.

The ordinary form of the 'drinking-cup' has a cylindrical neck which sometimes inclines to an inverted cone, joined to a globular body, both portions being covered with ornament, whereas the corresponding continental form, the *Schnur-becher*, has the body quite plain except for a fringe that serves as a border to the ornamented neck.   The sharp angle between the two component parts was not constant, and there are intermediate forms between the angular and the bell (or tulip) pattern that occurs in Germany and Holland as well as in the dolmens of Brittany and other parts. In all their varieties, however, 'drinking-cups' are on the Continent definitely assigned to the neolithic period, and it is without prejudice to their chronology that they are here noticed among the contents of Round barrows.

The ornament is for the most part disposed in horizontal bands, like the continental *Zonen-becher*, but in some cases the vertical treatment of the neck-ornament emphasises its distinction from the body.   It is executed by means of twisted thongs impressed in the moist clay, producing the characteristic cord-pattern, and also by pointed or shaped rods of bone or wood, forming herringbone or hatched patterns and stamped rings.   It may be added that though 'drinking-cups' are usually found in Round barrows with unburnt bodies, two examples were found in Yorkshire (Case 29) and the same number in Wiltshire associated with cremated remains, while this type of vessel is rarely found with articles of bronze.

2. *Food-vessels* (plate v, 4–9).   These undoubtedly succeeded the taller and better-made 'drinking-cups,' and are found in considerable numbers in Ireland as well as in Britain, the majority having been deposited with unburnt bodies in Round barrows, though they are frequently found among, and even containing, cremated human remains.   The ware is somewhat coarser than that of the class described above, and considerably thicker; while the ornament, which is lavishly bestowed on the outside of the vessel, extends in some specimens outside the lip, and a cruciform design is by no means uncommon on the bottom.   They are

sometimes provided with covers, and with a number of lugs or ears round the contracted neck, which are either pierced for the insertion of a cord, or are merely ornamental survivals of such attachments. The mouldings round the neck and rim and the delicate ornamentation on many specimens render the 'food-vessels,' on the whole, the most attractive class of Bronze age pottery in this country, and it is interesting to note that they are quite unrepresented outside the British Isles, having been developed locally and not introduced from abroad. A remarkable fact is that they are rare in Southern England and are entirely wanting in Wiltshire, a district otherwise rich in prehistoric remains.

3. *Cinerary urns* (plate v, 10–12). As a class these are un-doubtedly later than the 'drinking-cups' and 'food-vessels,' and formed receptacles for the cremated remains of the dead. The change in quality, design, and dimensions is very striking, and it is not surprising that many of these urns, being of considerable size as well as of coarse and ill-baked ware, have only been recovered in a very fragmentary condition. Their magnitude, however, says something for the technical skill of the potter, and the grit that is noticeable in the paste was necessary to prevent the clay from cracking during the process of firing. The usual form consists of two truncated cones placed base to base, the upper one forming a deep overlapping brim to which the orna-mentation is in many cases confined. Other shapes are, how-ever, common, and specimens from one or two sites have the walls almost vertical, while the decoration was executed with a twisted thong, with a pointed tool, or with the finger-point and finger-nail, the size of which suggests that the potters belonged to the female sex, as is generally the case among savages at the present day. In barrows cinerary urns occur either upright or inverted ; and in the latter case, there may have been a perish-able covering tied over the mouth to keep the bones inside, but that this was not the usual practice seems clear from the fact that the ornament would in that way be entirely hidden from view. Associated with cinerary urns, and sometimes placed within them, are commonly found the fourth class of vessels, which run to the other extreme, and are often very diminutive but highly ornamented.

4. *Incense-cups* (figs. 17, 21, 22, 38). The name of this division is again due to Colt Hoare, and though purely conjectural, may be retained till some more plausible explanation of their use is forthcoming. They are intimately associated with the burning of the dead, but are not by any means as common as cinerary urns, inside which they are very frequently found. In shape and decoration they vary considerably, but are generally pierced in one or more places as if to assist combustion. The more

characteristic forms are illustrated and many have loops for suspension, while in some cases the bottom is ornamented with cruciform and other designs similar to those already referred to on certain 'food-vessels,' but which are in all probability devoid of any special significance. As some specimens are unpierced, it is unlikely that they were used for incense, even if we suppose incense was then procurable, but the same objection is valid against their use as braziers to carry sacred fire from the family hearth to the funeral pyre ; and the perforations negative the idea that they were used as lamps. Whatever their use, they seem in nearly every case to have been placed in the grave after the body had been reduced to ashes. Though found throughout Britain and Ireland, they occur but rarely in Dorset and the neighbouring

Fig. 17.—'Incense-cup,' Roughridge Hill, Wilts. $\frac{2}{3}$

districts to the north and west, and so far as is known are altogether wanting on the Continent, though a few similar specimens are recorded from tombs in the Channel Islands.

Cases 12, 13.

The globular cinerary urn from Lambourn Downs, here illus-trated (fig. 18), belongs to a type found also in Dorset (Case 16), and has a chevron pattern barely discernible, as well as lugs or bosses round the shoulder. A specimen from Ashford (fig. 19), of similar form, shows a pair of holes bored near the brim to repair a crack before its deposit in the earth ; and other examples of this practice are shown from Middlesex, Dorset, Wilts. and Berks. (Case 15). This is one of an interesting series of urns shown here and below the main shelf in Cases 15–20. They were all found on the common between Ashford and Sunbury, Middlesex, arranged in straight lines running east and west or in crescents facing east, but no mounds were visible. Nearly all had been placed just below the surface in an inverted position, the consequence being that in most cases the bottom has been ploughed off and the upper part alone remains. The sides of most were nearly vertical (fig. 19), and the ornament consisted of a raised band a little below the rim, with finger-indentations or a few bosses in the same position. Two large hollows were found in which cremation had taken place, the ashes being subsequently transferred to the graves, where they were placed in, or covered by, the urns. No metal was found on this site, though about thirty burials were found in a space of 50 ft. by 20 ft.

Examples of the 'food-vessel' are here arranged to show the usual ornament on the inside of the rim ; and at the bottom of the Case are small vessels, from various parts, with ears or lugs, originally intended for suspension.

FIG. 18.—Cinerary urn, Lambourn Downs, Berks. ¼

The large cinerary urn with two handles, from an oval barrow at Tregaseal, near St. Just, Cornwall, was found inverted in a small cist and packed round with stones and rubbish. The cist was of dry masonry and adjoined a sepulchral chamber built in the same mound. This was formed of upright stone slabs, the interior being over 11 ft. long, 2 ft. wide, and 4 ft. high, with three large capstones, and was no doubt erected in neolithic times. Subsequent burials in and around it might account for the burnt bones, pottery, the perforated whetstone within the larger cist, and the added building at the end. The urn is remarkable not only for its size but also for a raised cross on the bottom inside, which may be compared with one from a cave near Brixham, in Case 16.

The cinerary vessel resembling a breakfast-cup was found by Mr. Borlase containing and surrounded by burnt human bones in a pit 9 ft. from the top of a barrow on Denzell Downs, near St. Columb, Cornwall. It is of exceptional form, and, unlike other sepulchral urns from the county, bore no traces of fire. Four urns, of which two are exhibited, were found at Clahar Garden, Mullion parish, in a cairn 36 ft. in diameter, which was enclosed by an outer ring of stones. The large four-handled urn from Tredinney was found inverted in a cist within a circular cairn, the latter being surrounded by a ring 38 ft. in diameter, formed of 16 granite blocks set on edge. The body had evidently been reduced to ashes on a flat stone above the cist, and the bottom of the urn may have been broken off to admit the cremated remains.

For **Case 14** see under Case 4 (p. 30).

Cases 15, 16.

Sepulchral pottery, mainly from Dorset, excavated by the late

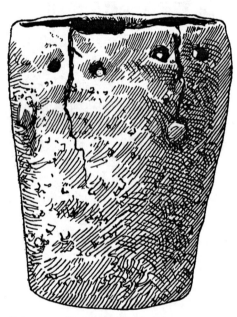

FIG. 19.—Cinerary urn with repair-holes, Ashford, Middlesex. ¼

Mr. Henry Durden, of Blandford. The Milborne barrow measured 10 ft. in height, and 160 ft. in circumference. At a depth of $2\frac{1}{2}$ ft. was a cairn of flints 2 ft. high, under which lay two skeletons on their backs, with the feet to the east. These interments may have been centuries later than the cremated remains found in another cairn at the centre of the mound, $4\frac{1}{2}$ ft. high, and 16 ft. from east to west. In this mass were found large urns with covers of flint or sandstone, and smaller vessels, indicating nearly fifty burials here.

A small series of 'food-vessels' from Scotland and Ireland, the latter (plate v, 4–6) showing certain peculiarities, and including a bowl-shaped variety (plate v, 5) confined to that island. It is on such that the ornamentation of the period reaches its highest development. In Co. Down more than fifty stone cists containing burnt bones were found in one cairn, and in the north-west angle of each cist was a 'food-vessel' containing a little blackish granulated earth.

Below are some decorated fragments of large vessels, probably of cinerary urns, found in one of the upper levels of a cave at Berry Head, Devon, not far from the famous Brixham Cave (Cases 121, 122, in iron gallery above). These were found above a stalagmite floor which covered plentiful remains of extinct animals. An interesting relic from this cave is a bone handle of some bronze

PLATE IV. BRONZE CAULDRON AND URN.

instrument which has left a greenish stain. An urn from Ashford has raised semicircles round the upper part that may possibly represent the handles of a basket prototype. Similar examples may be seen below Cases B and D.

Cases 17, 18.

In 1850 eight barrows were examined on Broughton Common, about 25 miles north of Lincoln. They had been much reduced by the plough, none being at that time more than 4 ft. high, and all were circular, with diameters of 60–80 ft. One of the cinerary urns is plain but well-fired, of a reddish colour, and

FIG. 20.—Sepulchral pottery : cairn near Swansea, Glamorganshire. ¼

contained among the burnt bones two flint lance-heads, one very well chipped, shown with others in Case F. Another barrow contained two urns, one inverted as a cover over the other, with a small tanged knife or razor of bronze among the ashes. The barrows contained one burial each, the urns being upright and often surrounded by charcoal and ashes, but not protected in any way by stones, the sole material being a sandy peat.

Five miles from Swansea, Glamorganshire, was a cairn 90 ft. in diameter and 4 ft. high, at a place called Mynydd Carn Goch (the Waste of the Red Cairn). Within the circumference was a ring of stones almost concentric, a few inches below the surface

E

of the mound. The largest vessel of the three (fig. 20) shown together was east of the centre, buried below the original ground-level, the interstices of the grave being filled with charcoal and the whole covered with a flat stone. The other urn was above the original surface, inverted on a flat stone; and the 'incense-cup' was near the western edge of the cairn. The bones were principally inside the urns, but throughout the cairn were large layers of charcoal, thickest in the vicinity of the burials.

Of the two urns from a barrow at Colwinston, in the same county, the taller was found near the centre on a stone slab,

FIG. 21.—'Incense-cup,' North Newbold, E. R. Yorks. ⅔

with other slabs built round and one placed on top. It was full of burnt bones, among which was a calcined bone pin, 2 in. long, with a large eye; pins of this kind were often used to fasten either a cloth in which the ashes were collected from the pyre, or the garment on the body before crema-tion. The other was 2 ft. distant, also protected by slabs of stone and a well-fitting cover, which shows that the skeleton of a mole and many lower jaw-bones and ribs of mice, which were found above the human ashes, were deposited in the urn before interment.

A group of three vessels was found in ploughing near Wycombe, Bucks., buried in a shallow grave in the chalk. The large cinerary urn at the top of the Case was inverted and contained an 'incense-cup' among the ashes; while the third vessel lay outside, resting on the shoulder of the urn, also inverted. These three vessels are in a vertical line to the left.

The mound in which two 'incense-cups' were found at North Newbold, East Riding of Yorkshire, was one of five, all being ori-ginally about the same size, 40 ft. in diameter and 4 ft. high. At a depth of about 15 in. was a hearth near the centre, filled with burnt bones, and on and amongst the ashes were the cups of which one is illustrated (fig. 21); but no other remains were found in this mound.

The 'incense-cup' from Beedon, Berks., was found 10 ft. deep with a cremated interment in the south side of a 'bell-barrow' called Borough (or Burrow) Hill. Below a layer of charred wood

in the centre of the mound was a ring of seven holes in the
original surface, about 1 ft. deep and 2 in. in diameter, partly
filled with charred or decayed wood (cf. Case 27). At Bulford,
Wilts., a remarkable specimen (fig. 22) was found in a barrow

FIG. 22.—'Incense-cup' and design on base, Bulford, Wilts. ⅔ and ¼

with a cinerary urn, two bronze pins and small beads; on the
bottom are deeply incised concentric rings closely resembling the
design often seen on 'cup-marked' stones (below Case C).

The ornamented cover (fig. 23) of a vase somewhat like that

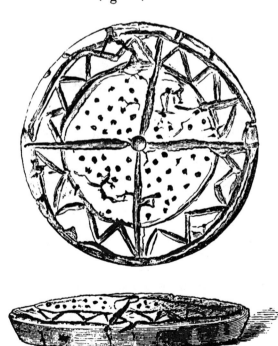

FIG. 23.—Cover of urn, Durnford, Wilts. ⅔

from Broughton, Hants (fig. 24), was found with cremated burials in one of seven barrows at Durnford, Wilts., and is of comparative rarity. 'Food-vessels' have been found with covers (fig. 30) in Yorkshire, and a remarkable casket with lid is shown in Case F.

Cases 19, 20.

On the main shelf is a series of 'drinking-cups' which may to a great extent date from the neolithic period, but should be noticed here as the earliest well-defined type of sepulchral pottery in the country. Special attention may be drawn to a specimen with handle from Appleford, Berks., found near the

Fig. 24.—Urn, Broughton, Hants. ⅔

shoulder of an adult skeleton. Another is exhibited in the adjoining Case 21 (plate v, 2), and others are known from Pickering, North Riding of Yorkshire; Brixworth, Northants., and March, Isle of Ely. The drinking-cup from Lambourn Downs, Berks. (plate v, 1), may be taken as a good example of one variety.

To the *right* of the Case are vessels from Wales, Scotland, and Ireland. One was found in a cist at Inchnacaorach, near Cawdor Castle, Co. Nairn, with three rude bone implements (fig. 25) in association with a crouching skeleton.

Among several examples from Suffolk may be mentioned a 'drinking-cup' (fig. 26) and vase found at Brandon with the bracer (bowman's wrist-guard) exhibited in Case F (fig. 95). No human bones, burnt or otherwise, were found with them, and it is therefore likely that they belonged to an unburnt burial, perhaps of the neolithic period (p. 55).

The series of vases from Hitcham, Bucks, was found during

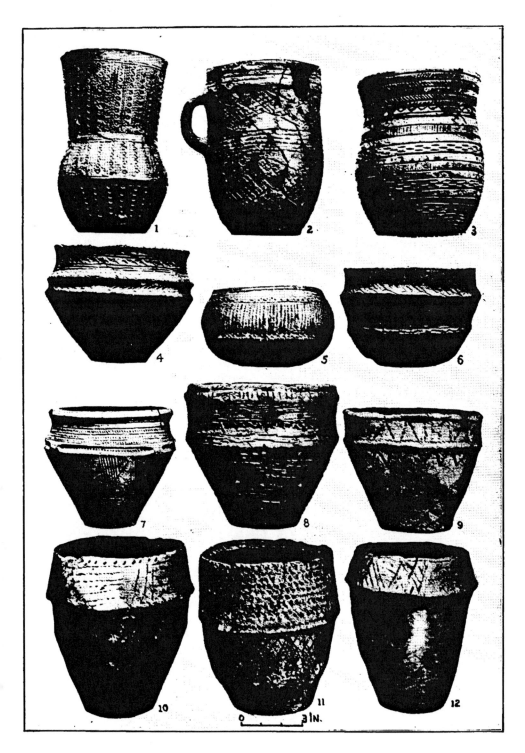

PLATE V. SEPULCHRAL POTTERY, BRITISH ISLES.
(Cases 12-30, *see* p. 41.)

the excavation of some circular dwellings in which 'drinking-cups,' cinerary urns, and other vessels (Case 13) are said to have come to light, together with bones of domestic animals, ornamented pottery fragments, and part of a polished stone axe. These hut-circles or pit-dwellings were formed by sinking a floor 3–7 ft., and throwing out the earth round the opening which was 14–20 ft. in diameter: on the bank thus formed were placed stakes leaning towards the centre and supporting a roof of turf, bracken, or other material. Similar dwellings have been found within the earthwork on Eggardun, Dorset.

GREENWELL COLLECTION: Cases 21–30.

The important excavations conducted by Canon Greenwell on

FIG. 25.—Urn and bone implements, Cawdor Castle, Co. Nairn. ⅓

the Yorkshire Wolds and elsewhere in England, and published by him in *British Barrows* and the *Archaeologia* lii. of the Society of Antiquaries, enable us to add some important details to the general account already given of the Bronze age burials. In the first place his discoveries have made it clear that the Long barrows owe their peculiar form not to accident, but to the sepulchral usages of a population previous to the introduction into this country of any metal except gold. Though the Yorkshire examples of this type contain human remains that were cremated on the spot in an elaborate manner, and those in Gloucestershire and north Wiltshire covered stone chambers in which unburnt bodies were deposited, it is evident that both groups are older than the Round barrows from which the present series of pottery is derived.

There are, however, within certain of the circular mounds coffin-shaped receptacles (stone cists) for the unburnt body (figs. 27, 28) ; and also enclosing-stones at or inside the margin of the mound (fig. 28) that recall the stone chamber and the ring-fence of the Long barrows. Canon Greenwell remarks that a very close connection thus appears to exist between the Long barrows and certain of the Round barrows of Britain which also agree in the absence of metal and the scarcity of pottery vessels in association with the interments. Attention has already been directed to the striking difference in the character of the skulls found respectively in the

Fig. 26.—' Drinking-cup,' Brandon, Suffolk. ⅔

Long and Round barrows (p. 19), and it is reasonable to suppose that the ' drinking-cups,' which are undoubtedly the earliest form of vessels from the Round barrows, are to be referred to the transition period when the population was mixed, and the long-skulled aborigines were giving way before short-skulled immigrants from the Continent.

In this connection fundamental differences in the disposal of the dead must also be noticed. The Long barrows contain both burnt and unburnt remains in different localities, but in the Round barrows not only do sepulchral vessels of pottery appear, but in cases of cremation the ashes of the dead were deposited either in a hollow in the floor of the grave or in a cinerary urn. Again, the unburnt body was laid on one side, right or left indifferently, and directed towards any point of the compass, with the knees almost invariably doubled up to the chin and the hands often in front of the face, but in no uniform position. It was, however, observed on the Yorkshire Wolds that when the head pointed approximately to the west, by far the larger number of bodies were laid on the right side, whereas when the head was to the east, the majority lay on the left side, the tendency being for the face to be set towards the mid-day sun.

Apart from subsequent or secondary interments, there were several instances on the Wolds of more than one body in a grave,

FIG. 27. Section of barrow, Bamborough, Northumberland (cxcvii).

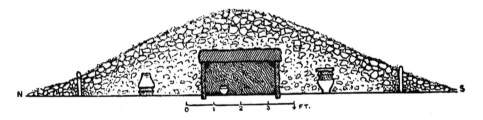

FIG. 28.—Section of barrow, Ford, Northumberland (clxxxvii).

and, on the other hand, barrows were sometimes met with in which no human remains could be discovered. In such cases it was argued, with great probability, that an unburnt interment had taken place and that owing to unfavourable conditions the bones had completely decayed ; for example, in sandy soil it is very rare to find any traces of buried bones even of much more recent date than the Bronze age, whereas burnt bones are practically indestructible. Some barrows have indeed been regarded as cenotaphs, or monuments raised to commemorate, but not to contain, the dead who were buried elsewhere. It is, however, probable that in some cases the skeleton, if not altogether decayed, has been overlooked by the explorer, especially as the principal interment is occasionally at some distance from the centre owing to the irregular construction of the mound.

Besides the potsherds and flint chippings already mentioned, fragments of charcoal were rarely, if ever, wanting in burials by inhumation examined by Canon Greenwell. This substance, in large or small quantities, was in actual contact with the body, and cannot therefore be merely the remains of the fire at which the funeral feast was cooked. As the rite of cremation was prevalent in this country during the Bronze period, it is not unlikely that in cases where the dead were not reduced to ashes, it was considered sufficient that the body should pass through the fire; and for this ceremonial act the application might at times have been so trifling as to leave upon the bones no indication of burning.

The manner in which the dead were deposited in the barrows varied considerably on the Wolds as elsewhere in this country; but in the North and East Ridings, as also in Derbyshire, the Round barrows were almost without exception bowl-shaped (figs. 27, 28). Sometimes the body, whether burnt or unburnt, had been placed in the mound without anything to protect it from the surrounding earth or stones; at other times, in a stone cist on or below the original level of the ground, in a hollowed tree-trunk, or in an oval or circular grave; while secondary interments occupied other parts of the mound at various levels. In most cases of cremation the body appears to have been burnt apart from the place where the bones were ultimately deposited; but numerous instances occur where the calcined remains had been interred on the site of the funeral pile, which was frequently constructed over a hollow made to contain the ashes. Pins, generally of bone, have been commonly found with deposits of burnt bones; in most cases they are themselves calcined, and no doubt belonged to the dress in which the body was enclosed before burning, but when untouched by fire they have probably served to fasten the cloth or hide in which the bones were collected after cremation. The care with which this was commonly done is well illustrated by Homer's account in the *Iliad* of Hector's white bones being gathered up from amongst the ashes of the pyre by his brethren and companions. The custom of sacrificing animals and human victims in honour of the dead may explain the traces of more than one human skeleton, and of bones of the ox (*Bos longifrons*), pig, goat or sheep, horse, and dog in cremated burials.

The green stain sometimes observable on bones from the barrows is not always due to the proximity of bronze or copper, but has been found on analysis to be caused by the presence of phosphate of iron, a salt which can assume various tinges of blue and green. There is, however, no doubt that a minority of the Round barrows on the Wolds contained, besides a large number of flint, bone, and horn implements, arms and ornaments, copper and bronze implements that fall into six well-defined classes.   All the conditions, however, point to the early date of such interments in the Bronze period, and the comparative scarcity of the metal.

The following figures for the Round barrows of the Yorkshire Wolds excavated by Canon Greenwell may be of interest. Altogether about 435 burials were discovered, burnt or unburnt, some being disturbed and scattered, others containing more than one body.   Of the total, seventeen had implements or ornaments of metal, some possibly of copper but usually described as bronze ; seventy-three had implements of flint or other stone ; and five had tools or ornaments of jet, bone, deer's horn, or boar's tusk. Of the unburnt burials, about 350 in all, about 23 per cent. were accompanied by articles of some kind, against 13 per cent. in the cremated burials.   Though bronze was no doubt well known during the later cremation period, economy of the still precious metal would account for the fact that it was absent in all but five cremated burials ; while the funeral fire explains the comparative rarity of more perishable articles in graves of the same description —11 per cent. against 19 per cent. in unburnt burials.   Only about 24 per cent. of the burials in these barrows were accompanied by articles of any kind ; and this fact is of importance in view of two opinions as to the motives that led to such deposits with the dead.   A belief that such might be of use in another world, or a superstitious dread of using what had belonged to the dead, may have given rise to the practice, but in either case it is difficult to understand why it was not more generally observed. That great care and labour were bestowed on the burial and the raising of the mound is evident on many grounds, and some of the objects found in the graves are quite new and to all appearance specially made for the occasion.

The projecting range of Cases 21–30 contains most of the Barrow-relics excavated and presented by Canon Greenwell.   In the upper part of these Cases is exhibited sepulchral pottery from Yorkshire and Northumberland, the Roman numerals on the plinth of each specimen indicating the number of the barrow described in *British Barrows*, from which it was taken.   Cases 21, 22 contain 'drinking-cups,' and Cases 23, 24, 27, 28 'food-vessels,' all found with unburnt burials.   In the centre Cases 25, 26 are vases of special forms, some of which may have been made for domestic purposes, some of the finer cinerary urns, and a number of 'incense-cups' ; while Cases 29, 30 contain, besides a number of cinerary urns at the back, two 'drinking-cups' (LXII) and several 'food-vessels' found with burnt burials.   In Cases 23–30 large cinerary urns are arranged below the main shelf ; and on the floor of Cases 25, 26 are picks of deer-antler similar to those from the neolithic flint-workings at Cissbury in Cases 125, 126 (immediately above, in the iron gallery), illustrated in the *Stone Age Guide*, fig. 84.

They were found in the material of the barrows, and doubtless served to excavate the graves in the chalk subsoil. Smaller objects, of flint, bone, jet, bronze or other material, are placed in glass-topped boxes on the main shelf and bottom of the Cases. First, on the main shelf, come remains from Long barrows, dating from the neolithic period, and including no metal objects; followed by Round-barrow antiquities from the north of England, arranged geographically, the largest group being from Rudstone, East Riding of Yorkshire (Cases 23, 24). A small series from Northumberland, Cumberland, and Westmorland is placed in Cases 29, 30, with pottery from Scotland below; while the lower part of Cases 21, 22 is devoted to the southern counties of England.

FIG. 29.—Design on base of 'food-vessel,' Alwinton, Northumberland. $\frac{1}{2}$

The pottery selected for illustration comprises a fine 'food-vessel' (pl. v, 7) from Alwinton, Northumberland (CCII. Case 28), with a cruciform pattern on the base (fig. 29). and a diminutive specimen, smaller than some 'incense-cups,' provided with a lid (fig. 30), from Ganton, East Riding of Yorkshire, found with another of the same kind between the skeletons of a man and a woman (XXI. Case 23). The cinerary urn found inverted on the lid of a cist at Bamborough (CXCVII. fig. 27) has a peculiar scalloped pattern round the neck (Case 28); and the 'drinking-cup' found with a skeleton within the cist is in Case 22. In the other barrow illustrated (CLXXXVII. fig. 28), the cist contained a 'food-vessel' (Case 28) near portions of the skull of a child about two years old; while one of the six cinerary urns which encircled the cist is shown

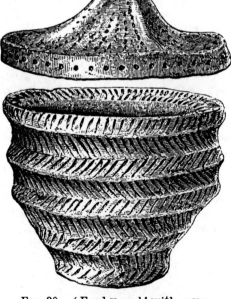

FIG. 30.—'Food-vessel' with cover, Ganton, E. R. Yorks. $\frac{3}{4}$

in Case 27. A well-made cinerary urn in miniature (fig. 31), with herring-bone decoration, was found with human remains which had been burnt on the spot, at Goodmanham, East Riding of Yorkshire

(LXXXIV. Case 30) ; and one of normal size (fig. 32) comes from what was no doubt a secondary interment in a barrow near Prudhoe, in Ovingham parish, Northumberland (CCXIV. Case 30). It much resembles a 'food-vessel' in outline and decoration, the latter covering the outside and extending within the lip.

The celt from Butterwick, East Riding of Yorkshire (XXXIX. Case 25), was found in a primary grave, and had evidently been slung from the waist of a young man, the wooden handle being traceable for nearly two feet. In his right hand had been held a bronze knife-dagger, of which the ox-horn handle and wooden sheath could be discerned, and above the dagger a flint knife, while below it was a bronze awl. On the breast were six buttons of jet and sandstone, with V-shaped perforations, used to fasten the dress. The grave was thus richly furnished ; and the form of the celt (fig. 33), evidently derived from a stone prototype, together with the absence of cremation, shows this to have been a burial of the early Bronze period, an analysis of the celt showing 87·97 per cent. copper and 10·74 per cent. tin. A dagger from Helperthorpe, East Riding of Yorkshire (XLIX. Case 28), gives the original proportions of the handle, though the ox-horn plates have

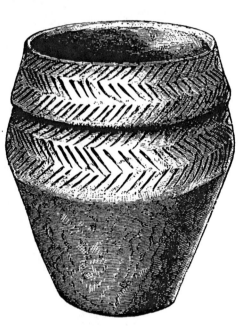

Fig. 31.—Cinerary urn, Goodmanham E. R. Yorks. ½

perished (fig. 34). The point of this, like that of the Butterwick dagger, was touching the chin of the skeleton ; and the blade was doubtless reduced to its present shape by repeated whetting.

Conical buttons of jet with V-shaped perforations are commonly found in Barrow deposits ; and are shown in the glass-topped boxes in Cases 21–30 as well as in Case F. They are often engraved on the top, and one illustrated from Rudstone, East Riding of Yorkshire (fig. 35), was found with other objects beside a male skeleton (LXVIII. Case 25). It is decorated with a cross, not an uncommon design at that period, and lay just under a jet ring (like fig. 36) with similar perforations from the circumference. The equivalent of a 'flint and steel'—a flint flake and nodule of iron pyrites (*Stone Age Guide*, fig. 130)—was found in the same grave near the skull. The jet ring (fig. 36) was also found resting on a button of the same kind at Thwing, East Riding of Yorkshire, on the right arm of a skeleton (LX. Case 23). Ornamented bone beads or buttons of another shape (fig. 37) are remarkably like those from Lake, Wilts. (Case F), which, however, are not perforated. The three with ornament lay at the right elbow of a young woman's skeleton at Folkton, East Riding of Yorkshire (LXXI. Case 28), while a plain one was found, with a bronze drill or awl, below the hips. The number

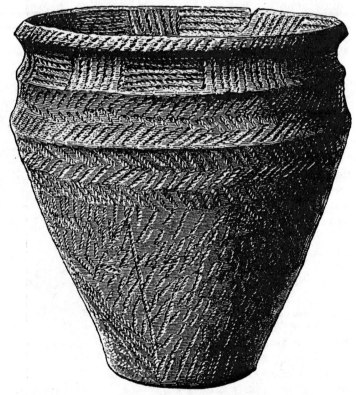

Fig. 32.—Cinerary urn, Ovingham, Northumberland. ⅓

is the same as at Lake, and the cruciform patterns in both cases were produced by burning the surface with a sharp-pointed instrument.

A barrow at Aldbourne, Wilts., contained an exceptional number of articles (in boxes below Case 21), which may be described in some detail as typical of the Round barrows generally. The mound was 90 ft. in diameter, and at the time of opening was still 6 ft. in height, though much ploughed down. It was composed of earth with some chalk and sarsen-stones, and contained at the centre a pile of sarsen-stones which had been exposed to fire. This 'cairn' was 28 ft. in diameter and 5 ft. high. Beneath it was a space from which the turf on the original surface level had been removed down to the chalk rock, and in the grave thus formed from north to south was a deposit of burnt bones underlaid with wood and covered by a layer of charcoal and

FIG. 33.—Primitive celt, Butterwick, E. R. Yorks. ½

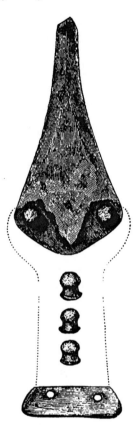

FIG. 34.—Knife-dag-
ger with remains of
handle, Helperthorpe,
E. R. Yorks. ½

wood-ashes, no doubt collected from the funeral pile. At the south end lay the 'incense-cup' (Case 25, fig. 38) and what seems to have been its cover. Both these parts were found much broken but in a clayey mass together; and the lower portion is very similar to one from Beckhampton, Wilts. (Case 17). The ware is good but soft, and the ornament, which extends also to the bottom and the inside of the cover, is characteristic of the period. The upper part is, however, much thicker, rather clumsy as a cover, and evidently intended for suspension, as the

knob is pierced.   Among the burnt bones were also pieces of
a small bronze knife and of two bronze awls, all having apparently
passed through the funeral fire.   Seven beads were also found,
three of pale-green glass-paste (like fig. 97), two of amber, a
barrel-shaped specimen of lignite, and one made from the stem of

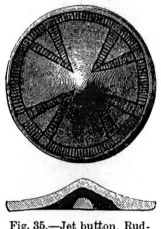

Fig. 35.—Jet button, Rud-
stone, E. R. Yorks.

Fig. 36 — Jet ring,
Thwing, E. R. Yorks.

an encrinite.   Close to the beads was a large flat ring of lignite,
a pendent ornament of the same material, a conical button of
shale, a cast of a cardium shell, and a small polished pebble of
haematite.   A few inches beyond the north end of the grave
was another 'incense-cup' with a few scattered burnt bones, with

Fig. 37.—Bone beads, Folkton, E. R. Yorks.

similar ornament but of inferior fabric.   It had, however, a peculiarity of very rare occurrence in this country.   The decorative
incisions, produced probably by a bronze pricker, have been filled
in with some white material like finely powdered chalk, probably
applied in a semi-liquid state, like the 'slip' of Roman and later
times.
     Among the ashes covering the bones were six unburnt flint
flakes, and among the sarsen-stones of the cairn were many

bones of ox and pig, some teeth of oxen, two flint arrow-heads, one being barbed and unburnt, the other triangular and partially calcined; and the end of a boar's tusk which had apparently been fashioned. In the earth above the cairn were nine sherds of pottery, including two pieces of large thong-marked vessels, and part of a 'drinking-cup' filled in with white like the 'incense-

FIG. 38. —'Incense-cup' with cover, Aldbourne, Wilts. $\frac{2}{3}$

cup' just mentioned, and some flakes and chippings of flint, all unburnt.

Much the same might be said about the material of other Round barrows in this country. There are often signs of earlier interments with unburnt human bones (here indicated by the 'drinking-cup'), and relics of what may be regarded as the funeral feast, where the ox and pig were the usual viands, the bones generally split for the extraction of the marrow. Chips of flint, arrow-heads, &c., may have been lying on the surface when the adjoining soil was thrown up to form the barrow.

A small series of sepulchral pottery from Scotland is exhibited in the lower part of Cases 29, 30. The two cinerary urns from Tealing, Forfarshire, were found within a barrow above a stone cist which contained a crouching male skeleton with cephalic index of 73, clearly dolichocephalic (p. 19). It is possible that the burnt and unburnt burials were in this case contemporary. At Kilmartin, Argyllshire, a cairn 110 ft. in diameter and 13½ ft. high, was surrounded by two incomplete rings of standing stones and enclosed two cists, the primary at the centre containing no human bones except traces of unburnt burials and a 'food-vessel' covered with ornament, and resembling some from the same part of Scotland and from Ireland in Cases 15, 16. The 'drinking-cup' from Ballymenach, near Kilmartin, was found in a disturbed cist within a mound 95 ft. in diameter, near cup-marked stones ; the fragments lying mixed with unburnt bones in sand and gravel. The third vessel from this neighbourhood is a bowl like one from Heslerton, East Riding of Yorkshire (Case 26), and was found in a chambered cairn on Largie Farm, originally 134 ft. in diameter. The central cist was over 19 ft. long, nearly 4 ft. wide and 9½ ft. high, the sides, walls, and roof being formed of large slabs of chlorite schist, with smaller stones in the interstices. Four compartments had been formed by three vertical cross-slabs 2½ ft. high ; and in the compartment at the south end, which had an altar-like slab raised from the floor (as at Tregeseal, Cornwall, Case 12), the bowl lay near a small cist in an undisturbed layer of dark matter and burnt bones.

GERMANY : Cases 31–35.

The pottery exhibited here is remarkable both for its variety in form and its excellent manufacture. It is generally of a yellow colour and of thin, well-baked ware, superior to that found in this country. The collection was made by Dr. Klemm of Dresden, and is derived from various sites in Saxony and Lower Lausitz.

Two groups of urn-fields dating from the Bronze age are distinguished in this area, and of these the first is characterised by vases with conical bases (*Buckel-urnen*, plate vi, 2) ; by oval-bodied vases with spreading lip (13) ; and by a doubly conical form, the upper part deeper than the base (1), and decorated with incised lines. The second group comprises various shapes, which are frequently ornamented by fluting (6, 10, 12), while the inside of the rim is sometimes facetted as in our own 'food-vessels.' Linear ornament consists mainly of concentric semicircles and hatched triangles (5, 9), while one example on the plate (4) has besides this ornament a thin partition which is characteristic of the group. It has been thought that the *Buckel-urnen* and derivatives are the

PLATE VI.   SEPULCHRAL POTTERY, FROM THE CONTINENT.

(Cases 31-36, *see* p. 64.)

earlier; but, according to Prof. Deichmüller of Dresden, it may be that the difference is merely geographical—the first group occurring in the urn-fields of east and north-east Saxony, while the second belongs to the west and north-west, and is related to the Bronze age ware of West Germany. The second group is said not to occur in East Saxony, but both are represented in the Elbe valley. A bell-shaped beaker from the neighbourhood of Buda-Pesth is included in the plate (7) as a prototype of one form of 'drinking-cup' in this country, though itself doubtless of the neolithic period. Another form of 'drinking-cup' bears a remarkable resemblance to an early example from Merseburg (8), and is well represented in Cases 19, 22.

Antiquities of bronze from Germany are in Case G (p. 95).

DENMARK: Case 36.

Most of the Danish pottery belonging to the Bronze age was found in graves of the later period, though some definite types, represented by two examples in this Case, occur in neolithic times. Nearly all served as receptacles for the human ashes gathered from the pyre, and were no doubt in many cases manufactured expressly for the purpose. Very few of those exhibited display any artistic qualities, but the type with handle and columnar foot is of fine black paste. On the other hand, a rough handled vase (pl. VI, 11), resembling in form a certain number found in Britain (p. 52), is of inferior quality and ornamentation. The better forms, with well-marked profile, are connected with Central Germany, while the inferior types are more strictly local; but it is hardly possible to divide them chronologically. Only a very few examples can be referred to the early Bronze period, and it is probable that the increased output was due to the introduction of cremation (p. 104). For bronze objects see Case H.

SPAIN: Cases 37–39.

This series of well-made burial urns and vases well represents the large number found by MM. Siret in the south-east of Spain. Further remarks on these important discoveries will be found in the description of Case K (p. 130); but the pottery, from El Argar and other Bronze age sites, may here be treated separately. It reveals a surprising skill in modelling when it is remembered that the wheel was still unknown; and betrays an exceptional feeling for beauty of form. The ware is principally dark grey in colour and unornamented, some vessels being rounded at the base (fig. 39) and requiring a ring, perhaps of clay or esparto grass, to enable them to stand upright; others having elongated feet, which give them a very graceful appearance (fig. 39). High feet of a similar kind are known from other primitive sites within the Mediterranean area, such as Hissarlik (Troy) and Lengyel in Hungary (p. 101), and their prototypes are perhaps to be sought in Egypt. The dead were interred in a contracted position beneath the floors of the houses, the bodies being either protected by stone cists, or inserted in large urns of red ware (fig. 40) laid on their sides. The last was the favourite method, and the urns were either sealed by stone slabs or closed by being placed together in pairs mouth to mouth. It is almost certain that the corpse was inserted soon after death while the flesh still adhered to the bones, for the imprint of skin has been remarked upon rings and bracelets, while hair as well as traces of clothing have been found. The custom of urn-burial without cremation is another of the features which point to an influence from the East, for examples of this method of disposing of the dead are known at Biskra in Algeria, at Bargia Verezzi in Italy, in the Thracian Chersonese, in Asia Minor, and in Chaldaea; it is interesting to note that in the New World it also occurs in California, New Mexico, Nicaragua and Brazil. But on the whole the industry of El Argar is thought to bear a more local and indigenous character than that of the period which preceded it.

Fig. 39.—Sepulchral pottery, Almeria, Spain. ⅛

Fig. 40.—Interior of burial urn, Almeria. 1/10

The difficulty of making vessels of such large proportions as the burial-urns was met by moulding them in two portions which were joined while the clay was still moist. Traces of the joining are visible on both the examples exhibited; and smaller vessels were also moulded in the ground or other matrix (fig. 41), and baked possibly by burning wood inside. The upper part of the vases on high feet were sometimes used alone (fig. 39), while the inverted foot served as a cup, the form being imitated in the manufacture of complete specimens.

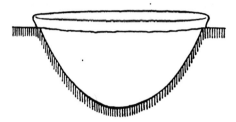

Fig. 41.—Section showing manufacture of bowl, El Argar, Almeria. ⅟₅

Other objects in Cases 38, 39 are pounding-stones for grain, a piece of burnt wattle-and-daub showing the material used for huts, also casts of bronze objects and of a skull with reversed diadem and ear-ornaments as found in an urn (fig. 40). The open celt-mould could only be used for copper. not for bronze.

INDIA : Cases 47, 48.

The great southern peninsula has been regarded by more than one archaeologist as the first home of the Bronze industry, but reasons have already been given to show that the theory is as yet unsupported by sufficient evidence: we have here to consider the principal discoveries of early metal implements or weapons which have hitherto been recorded.

The most remarkable of these was made in 1870 at Gungeria, about forty miles from Boorha, Mhow Taluk, Balaghat, Central India, where more than 400 flat celts (plate VII) and a number of thin silver ornaments (fig. 42), some circular, others cut into the outline of the heads of oxen, were found together. Analysis of some specimens showed that the metal was not bronze but copper, and this fact, supported by analysis of other implements from different localities in the Calcutta Museum, is held to prove the existence of a primitive copper stage in Hindustan. Doubts have been cast, however, on the extreme antiquity of the Gungeria find, partly because the silver ornaments are not very primitive in appearance, partly because the existence of two distinct forms among the celts suggests previous stages of development. The flat shape certainly does not prove as much as it would in Europe, for in Asia there is no evolution from the flat type through the winged to the socketed celt. On the other hand, silver has already been met with at a very early time in Spain and the Mediterranean, and some of the earliest Irish celts resemble the Gungerian examples. Another interesting discovery, also represented in the collection, took place at the beginning of last century at Niorai, Etawah. between the Ganges and the Jumna. Here swords and barbed lance-heads (Case K) of almost pure copper came to light; but objects of the same form now in the National Museum of Antiquities at Edinburgh, proved on analysis to contain 3·83 and 6·74 per cent. tin. Similar weapons are reported to have been found near Mathura (on the Jumna above Agra) and elsewhere. In addition to these objects, axes, armlets, and a lance-head were found in 1868 at Mynpuri in the North-west Provinces.

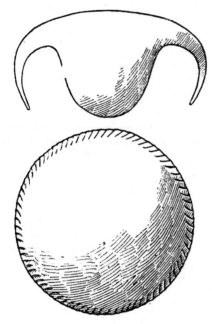

Fig. 42.—Silver ornaments, Gungeria, Balaghat, Central India. ⅓

Case A.

The *West* side of this Case contains spear-heads, daggers, swords and smaller objects from the Thames, a large proportion being from Taplow, Bucks. The spear-heads belong to the two main types, more fully dealt with under Case D, but the frequency of the flattened loop just beyond the base of the blade should be noticed. The longest specimen measures 22 in., and a remarkable example of the Irish type with small openings in the blade is illustrated (fig. 44). The most noteworthy object in the Case is a long spear-head (fig. 45), with gold studs near the bottom of the blade, recently found at Taplow. The socket has been broken, but it retains one of a pair of loops and originally had a total length of about 24 in. It is of comparatively early date, and is obviously derived from a common form of dagger exhibited next to it, a socket having been added for use on a shaft and the studs no doubt representing the rivets on the base of the prototype. Pointed blades, called

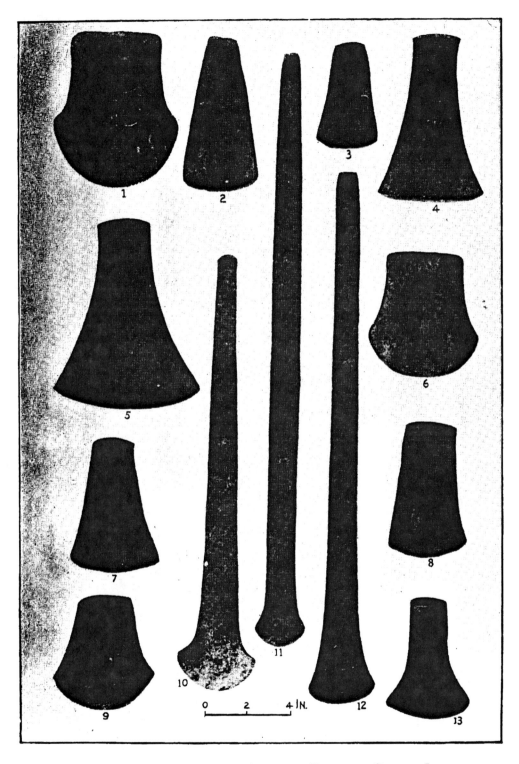

PLATE VII. COPPER IMPLEMENTS, GUNGERIA, BALAGHAT, CENTRAL INDIA.
(Cases 47, 48, *see* p. 67.)

knives, knife-daggers, or rapiers, according to their length, are well
represented, the handles being fixed by
means of a tang or rivets. A notable
example of the Italian terramara type (fig.
48) was no doubt imported through France.
A good sword-blade, ornamented pin (fig.
49), spear-head with remains of shaft, and
palstave (fig. 50), were found together near
the mouth of the Wandle. For more
perfect swords and other objects from the
Thames, see the upper part of Cases 6, 7 ;
and for types of sickles more usual in these
islands than that from Taplow (fig. 67), see
Case D.

On the *East* side are weapons from
Scotland, Wales, and the Thames. From
Aberdeenshire a group of two swords,
pin with disc-head turned over on the
stem, and chape like fig. 14. The globular

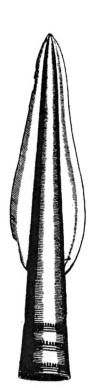

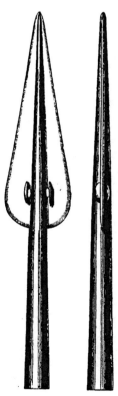

Fig. 43.—Spear-head, Thames at Thames Ditton ½

Fig. 44. — Perforated spear-head, Thames. ¼

Fig. 45. — Spear-head with gold studs, Thames at Taplow.

pommel on one of the swords occurs more than once in Scotland, but is rare elsewhere, though spherical pommels of bone, &c., must have been fairly common. A similar pin was found with swords of this and other kinds at Edinburgh. A find from Merionethshire contained types also found in the Thames, and the resemblance of a tanged chisel from Ty Mawr and a cylindrical chape from Montgomeryshire to specimens on the other side of the Case should be noticed. The socketed knife from Glamorganshire recalls several Irish specimens in Case C, and the form is common in France.

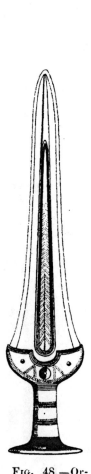

FIG. 46.—Dagger-blade, Thames at Richmond. ⅓

FIG. 47.—Dagger-blade, Thames at Thames Ditton. ⅓

FIG. 48.—Ornamented dagger, Thames. ¼

FIG. 49. Pin, Thames near mouth of Wandle. ¼

To the *right* is a collection of celts purchased from a marine-store dealer long ago, but there is no record of localities. A series from the Thames includes an ornamented flat celt of Irish type, palstaves and socketed celts of various sizes. Special mention should be made of one with different designs on the two faces from Kingston (fig. 51).

Case B.

It was formerly a common impression that the bronze of pre-Roman times came to this country from abroad, as was undoubtedly the case in Scandinavia; but the existence of moulds in this country, together with an ample supply of the constituent metals, shows that bronze was from the first manufactured on the spot. It is in fact likely that foreign traders in metal were first attracted to Cornwall and other parts by the knowledge that bronze was already in use among the natives, who had discovered the ores and the secret of smelting and combining them. It was not only in the production of the best metal for their purposes (a mixture of nine parts of copper to one of tin), that the British native showed his skill, but also in the difficult task of hollow-casting by means of a core. The flat open moulds of stone (Dorset and Northumberland, below Case D, and Spain, Case 39) were unsuited for casting anything but unalloyed copper, and it is

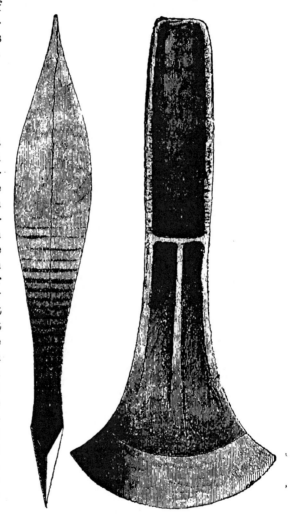

Fig. 50.—Palstave, Thames near mouth of Wandle. $\frac{2}{3}$

conceivable that these were resorted to during any temporary scarcity of tin ; but it is more probable that the open moulds represent, in this country and abroad, the earliest attempts at casting, which are far removed from the masterpieces produced at a later period. The existing moulds for swords, spear-heads, celts, &c., show that very little trimming was necessary after the operation of casting; but it must be remembered that the majority of moulds were no doubt of clay or compact sand, which have perished or been overlooked in excavations. The use of clay is well illustrated by a mould in this Case (fig. 52). It is of bronze, but was evidently itself cast in a mould of clay, which was formed round a model palstave and bound to it by twine reproduced in the metal.

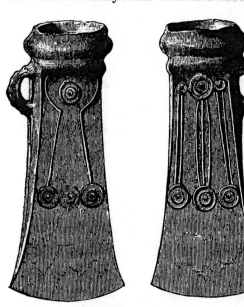

On the *left* of the *West* side are moulds in bronze and stone, as well as several casts of originals preserved in other collections. A rectangular block, with half-moulds for looped spear-heads and small pointed objects on the four faces, is illustrated (fig. 53) ; and the method of making the rivet-holes by casting is clear from the cross-bar in some of the moulds. The reproduction of a mould for a sword-hilt from Italy shows the method

FIG. 51.—Socketed celt, Thames at Kingston. ½

of hollow-casting. The core was in this case of bronze, but was generally of clay or sand, and in some instances remains of such cores may be seen in castings where the design or utility of the object is not thereby impaired.

To the *right* of the Case are long ingots of copper produced by running the molten metal into grooves cut in stone. Rude lumps of copper, like those from a founder's hoard at Grays Thurrock, Essex, are common, but tin is rarely included in these finds, and it is not present in the rough lumps which are about $98\frac{1}{2}$ per cent. copper, doubtless because the powdery ore is of a brown colour and not easily distinguishable in the ground. The two round cakes of bronze were perhaps used as anvils on which to beat out and harden the cutting-edges of implements by means of hammers like figs. 6, 69 and 70.

The leaden socketed celt from Seamer Moor was no doubt used as a model for the production of clay moulds; and the bronze mould from the Southall hoard here shown contained when found the remains of a similar leaden celt.

On the *East* side of the Case are models showing the various methods of hafting metallic celts. The illustration of an original handle (fig. 54) for a winged celt or palstave, shows the use of the prong; and the method of securing the head by a ligature through the loop may be seen in other examples.

Case C.

West Side. Two finds here are of special interest as including the predecessor of the spear-head, approximately dated by

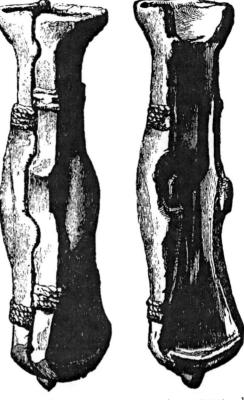

Fig. 52.—Bronze mould for palstaves, Wilts. ½

the presence of flanged celts, with rudimentary stop-ridge. Sixteen implements in all were found 1 ft. below the surface on Arreton Down, Isle of Wight, in 1735, the celts laid in order on the tanged weapons, which may be called daggers or spear-heads.

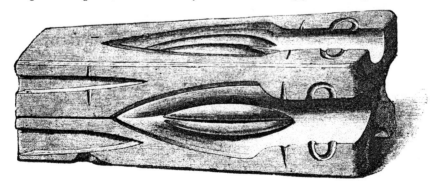

Fig. 53.—Stone mould for spear-heads, Lough Gur, Co. Limerick. ½

Several examples (fig. 55) have been found since, chiefly in the south of England, and one is said to have come from Italy; but they may be regarded as a local adaptation of the riveted knife-dagger, a decorated example of which was also found on Arreton Down. In 1868 sixteen celts, three daggers, another two-edged weapon, and a chisel, were found piled upon a ledge of rock under a heavy stone slab, two feet below the surface in a field at Plymstock, Devon (fig. 56). The close resemblance to the

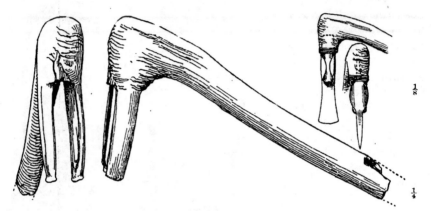

FIG. 54.—Handle of celt, with method of hafting, Hallein, Salzburg, Austria.

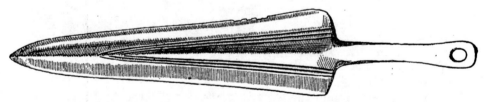

FIG. 55.—Tanged dagger, Hintlesham, Suffolk.   ½

Isle of Wight specimens will be noticed, and the relative date is confirmed by the flanged celts. A further point to be noticed is the occurrence in a barrow at Snowshill, Gloucestershire, of a stout tanged blade with incomplete cylindrical handle of bronze (fig. 71), like one actually included in the Arreton Down hoard. The Snowshill burial was primary, and by inhumation, containing also a knife-dagger with rivets, a bronze pin, and a stone axe-hammer, for which last compare Case F. A tanged knife from Sutton Courtney, Berks., perhaps represents an earlier stage of development, and belongs to a type occasionally found in barrows.

Nine examples of what are generally called arm-rings, but are very ill suited to the purpose, are here shown (fig. 57) from the Brighton Downs, Sussex, or neighbourhood. Examples in gold are said to have been found near Eastbourne; and it is possible that their manufacture was exclusively local. They occur with a palstave and a twisted bronze collar, the latter having on it when found spiral coils of bronze generally known as ring-money (cf. fig. 145). Plain armlets have also been found with them, and a decorated armlet of the usual shape is illustrated (fig. 58).

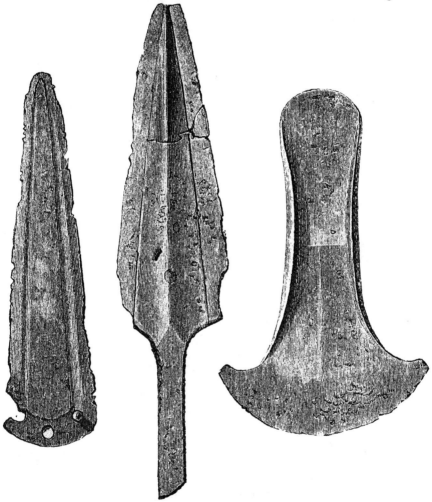

FIG. 56.—Part of hoard, Plymstock, Devon. ⅔

Eight torcs (twisted metal collars) from various sites in Dorset are all of the same type, with a double hook for fastening.

From Ireland come several daggers and rapier-blades, with rivet-holes or notches for attaching the handle, and a number of socketed knives and short swords (fig. 59), which are unusually common in that island ; a similar knife from the Minster hoard is shown on plate III. The halbert-blade is also characteristic, and nine examples are shown, some retaining their rivets (fig. 60). These weapons belong to the opening of the Bronze age, and

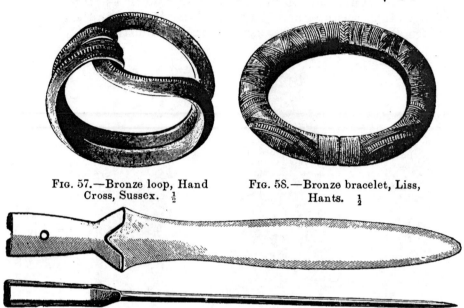

Fig. 57.—Bronze loop, Hand Cross, Sussex. ½

Fig. 58.—Bronze bracelet, Liss, Hants. ½

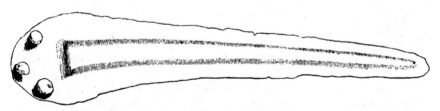

Fig. 59.—Socketed short-sword, Dungiven, Co. Derry. ⅓

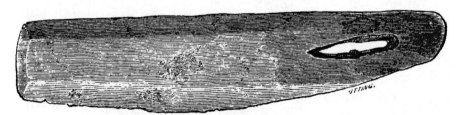

Fig. 60.—Halbert-blade, Slieve Kileta Hill, Co. Wexford. ¼

Fig. 61.—Knife, Cothill, Abingdon, Berks.

smaller examples have been found in Spain (fig. 126), though one of truly Irish appearance may be seen in Case J, from Cremona, Italy. A razor from Ireland, with the peculiar notch at the top of the blade, belongs to a type more common on the Continent, and the blade from Cothill, Berks. (fig. 61), may be a copy of the later form of razor common in Scandinavia (fig. 109).

East Side. Bronze swords found in the British Isles have handles cast in one piece with the blade, and belong either to the latest Bronze age or to the earlier half of the Hallstatt period. Such is the latest continental classification ; but it must be borne in mind that the Hallstatt period is barely represented in this country, and there is nothing to show that these swords did not continue in use here till the Late Keltic times, which roughly correspond to the La Tène period of the Continent.

Some idea of the complete sword can be gained from the cast exhibited here of a specimen found in Yorkshire. The original has evidently been moulded after a leaf-shaped sword like some in this Case, which had horn or bone plates attached by rivets to either side of the handle, and a heavy pommel of some kind, probably globular. Two swords have indeed been found in Northumberland with remains of leaden pommels of this shape, and some of those exhibited would be very

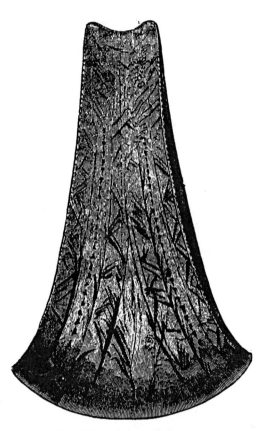

Fig. 62.—Flat celt, Co. Tipperary. $\frac{1}{2}$

ill-balanced weapons without such a counterpoise. How this was attached to the common expanded termination of the handle may be seen in the Tarves sword in Case A. which only lacks the plates of the grip.

The main varieties of the leaf-shaped type are illustrated on plate VIII, nos. 1–3, 5–7, and a general resemblance will be noticed in specimens from the Thames (Cases 6, 7) and Ireland (Cases 2–4), and those from various parts in this Case. The rivets sometimes passed through circular holes in the handle and base of the blade, and sometimes through slots in the handle (no. 2).

In many instances (plate VIII, nos. 1–3, 6) there are two notches near the base of the blade, for which no adequate reason has yet been given. The wooden scabbards then in use might be affected by the weather, so that the blade could not be pushed right home. Any risk of injury in that case would be avoided if the cutting-edges stopped short of the grip. This is another characteristic of the Hallstatt sword, and justifies the attribution of most if not all our specimens to the centuries between 800 and 400 B.C.

In the centre is a remarkably fine rapier-blade (plate VIII, no. 4)

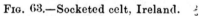

FIG. 63.—Socketed celt, Ireland. $\frac{2}{3}$

FIG. 64.—Mace-head, Great Bedwyn, Wilts. $\frac{1}{4}$

with its two rivets in position, found near Badbury Rings, a stronghold of the period in Dorset. This is much earlier than the swords, and should be compared with others from the Thames in Case A.

To the *right* is an example of a type common in Scandinavia, which has lost half its handle, but retains a metal grip secured by rivets to the base of the blade and by a tang that passed half-way up the hollow handle. A similar but complete specimen from Denmark is in Case H.

Plate IX shows the unusually large rivet-holes in the sword-fragment found at the foot of Beachy Head, with the winged celt and four gold bracelets (cf. p. 88); while another fragment recently acquired from a Kentish collection has the most unusual almond-shaped openings in the grip at the base of the blade, like a complete specimen found in Denmark, dating from the second period of Prof. Montelius (p. 103).

In the lower part of this Case, at the north end, are three ring-

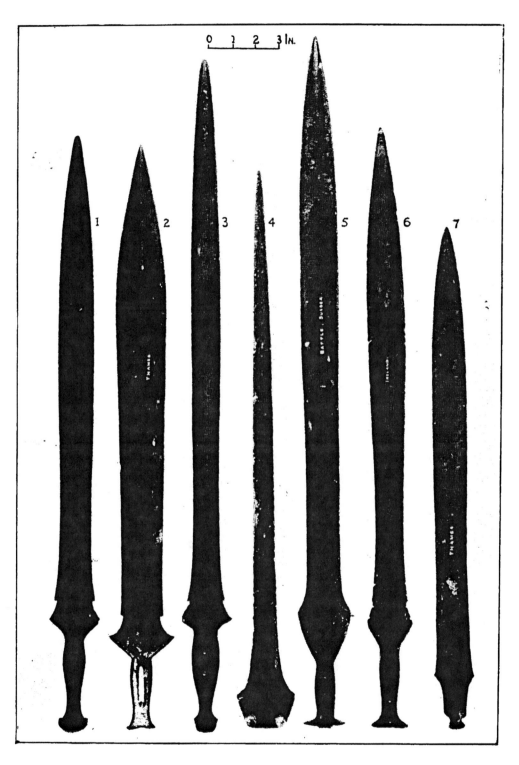

PLATE VIII. SWORDS AND RAPIER, BRITISH ISLES.
(Cases C, 6, 7, see p. 77.)

marked stones from the north of England, such as are frequently found in connection with burials of the Bronze age. These are sometimes included under the term 'cup-marked' stones, the simplest examples being merely pitted, and apparently dating from the neolithic period. The more elaborate markings, such as the concentric rings on two of those exhibited, and the rings with a radial groove on the third, are frequent in Northumberland, Yorkshire, Argyllshire, Kerry, and other parts of our islands; while they are

FIG 65.—Socketed celt, Beverley, E. R. Yorks. ⅔

FIG. 66.—Socketed celt, Thames near Wandsworth. ⅔

known also in India (Kumaon, Himalayas), North America (Maryland), Central America (Chiriqui), and New Caledonia (Paita). The rock-carvings of Scandinavia have been already referred to, and exhibit striking parallels; while cup-markings, with diameter of 2–3 in., are more widely spread, being specially frequent on erratic blocks in Central Europe. The significance of the geometrical designs is very uncertain, but a plausible hypothesis is that the rings, whether complete or interrupted, are connected with sun-worship; and their occurrence on the inner walls of burial cists and on sepulchral pottery (as the 'incense-cup', fig. 22), certainly favours that supposition.

Case D.

West Side. On the *left* are grouped ornamented flat celts (fig. 62) from the British Isles, and others remarkable for various reasons, arranged in types, for which see p. 40.   The diamond or cable-pattern on the sides (as opposed to the faces) of several flanged specimens should be noticed.   At the back are a few examples of the winged celt, a type rare in these islands but common on the Continent. An untrimmed palstave found near Harlech is shown here; and a socketed celt from Wales, as it left the mould, in the adjoining section.

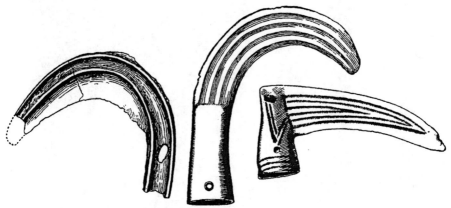

Thames at Taplow, Bucks.   Ireland.   Athlone, Co. Westmeath.
Fig. 67.—Bronze sickles, tanged and socketed.   ¼

To the *right*, socketed celts varying both in form and ornamentation: among them should be noticed a type resembling a modern axe (fig. 63), practically confined to Ireland, as are also the diminutive socketed celts shown here and in Case 3.   A number of maceheads (fig. 64), generally referred to the Bronze age, may be compared with others from Italy in Case J and in the Department of Greek and Roman Antiquities (Bronze Room, Wall-Case 15). The peculiar celt from Beverley (fig. 65) is not an isolated specimen, but is rare in England, and may be compared with some from France in Case E (fig. 84).   The socketed celt from Wandsworth is altogether exceptional (fig. 66); and on one from Dunmow, Essex, may be seen the survival of the wings of the earlier type (cf. fig. 16, no. 3).   Two double-looped palstaves, from Cornwall and Somerset, resemble specimens from Spain (Case K); but sickles with sockets (fig. 67, Irish), appear to belong, with only two or three exceptions, to these islands, the common continental type resembling that from Taplow, Case A.   Chisels are of various types (fig. 68), tanged or socketed, but gouges (c) are all of one class, with socket. Two groups from Lusmagh, Ireland, and Thorndon, Suffolk, are interesting as showing the tools in use at the same period.

East Side. The collection of bronze spear-heads in this Case is intended to illustrate the development of one group from the tanged dagger known as the 'Arreton type' (examples in Case C), and the various forms assumed by the leaf-shaped pattern. To the *left* are a number of spear or lance-heads characterised by converging ribs; by a pair of loops below, or a pair of openings in, the blades; and by the absence of rivet-holes in the socket. It will be noticed that a large proportion is from Ireland; and the investigations of Mr. George Coffey, whose classification is here followed in part, seem to justify the conclusion that this type was invented in Ireland, and in the course of its development spread to England and Scotland. It is extremely rare in France (Case 75), and almost unknown elsewhere, so that it is quite unconnected with the leaf-shaped pattern, which is almost universal.

The dagger is known to have been one of the earliest of bronze implements, and an advance on the most primitive form is shown by

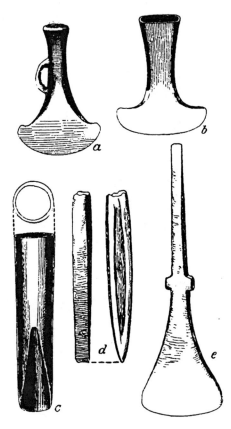

FIG. 68.—Chisels and gouge, England and Ireland. ½

several of the 'Arreton type,' which have tangs, perforated at the extremity, to pass through a handle (fig. 55). A specimen found with the others on Arreton Down, with a socketed bronze handle attached by rivets to the blade, and another from a Round barrow (fig. 71) appear to be prototypes of the Irish spear-head. The next stage is marked by the manufacture of spear-heads in one piece, the utility of a dagger-like weapon on the end of a shaft having been suggested in the interval. Provision was now made in the mould for a pair of loops to secure the head to the shaft by a ligature, and the result was the primitive type, fig. 72, examples of which are rare. ·The socket was gradually deepened, and encroached on the central rib, which, starting with the smaller ribs from the original junction of blade and handle, is often found well marked and angular. The tendency was for the cutting edges to become straight and to meet at a wider angle (fig. 73), while the loops sometimes approached the base of the blades. Specimens have been found with the loops in the angles thus formed (fig. 74), and, according to one view, their ascent did not cease there. Small narrow openings, flanked by projections similar to the flat-

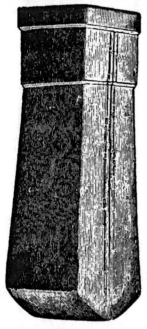

Fig. 69.—Hammer,
Thorndon, Suffolk.

Fig. 70.—Hammer,
Ireland.

tened loops seen on the socket, are found at various points in the broader part of the blade on either side of the central ridge; and these openings in time become larger and often crescent-shaped, while the projections disappear (pl. ii, 1). One of this last pattern is known from Central Russia. It is, however, by no means improbable that the openings in the blade were due in the first place to imitation of an early form of spear-head found in the second city at Hissarlik (2500–2000 B.C.) and in the Greek Islands, where the flat blade was inserted in a cleft stick bound by a cord passing through the openings (fig. 118). This type may well have been transmitted by sea from the Eastern Mediterranean early in the Bronze age, and it may be noticed that holes, perhaps relics of larger openings, are found at the base of the blade in several spear-heads from Italy (Case J), and in a remarkable specimen from France (fig. 136). Throughout this development the method of fastening by means of rivets through the socket was not generally adopted, but a few specimens in this Case show rivet-holes in the socket with either openings in the blade or loops on the socket.

The leaf-shaped spear-head with socket and rivet-holes is the more usual form in England, and is almost universal on the Continent. Particular attention is drawn to the patina '

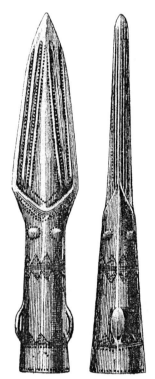

FIG. 71.—Dagger, barrow at Snowshill, Gloucs. ½

FIG. 72.—Spear-head, probably from Ireland. ½

FIG. 73. — Spear-head, Ireland. ½

on that from Fenny Bentley (fig. 75), found with two bronze pins, not so common in this country as elsewhere.

The discovery in Heathery Burn Cave, Co. Durham, is most important in many ways. It is by far the most instructive of any Bronze age deposit in this country not of a sepulchral character, and comprises the entire equipment of a family who had lived or taken refuge in the cave, and had there been apparently overwhelmed. The various objects may therefore be regarded as contemporary, and they unquestionably belong to the time when the Bronze age culture had reached its highest point in Britain.

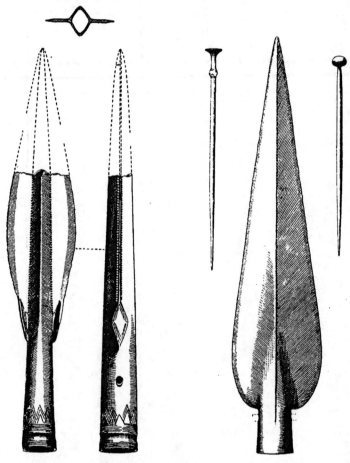

FIG. 74.—Spear-head, Brigmerston Down, Wilts. ⅓

FIG. 75.—Spear-head and pins,
Fenny Bentley, Derbyshire. ⅓

A spear-head, doubtless from this cave, is here shown with a pair of massive armlets (fig. 76), and a disc with three (originally four) loops on the back (fig. 77). Close parallels to other objects discovered—the knife, both tanged and socketed, the razor, socketed celt, and gouge—may be seen in the Dowris hoard (Case 2); and a large bronze cauldron found in the cave resembles that from Battersea in the lower part of Case 14, while part of the Dowris hoard was found in a cauldron. Chisels, awls, pins, and rings of ordinary types were also found, with a bronze mould for socketed celts, tongs, and runners, showing that metal was worked in the cave. One of the bronze bracelets exactly resembles that from Heneglwys in Case F, and of the two gold ornaments one was a massive armlet of an ordinary type, the other a hollow

Fig. 76.—Armlet, Heathery Burn Cave, Stanhope, Co. Durham. ⅓

Fig. 77.—Back of disc, Heathery Burn Cave. ⅓

penannular ring of triangular section. The only important classes of implements not represented in the find were the dagger, shield, hammer, and sickle.

Barbed spear-heads like that from Essex (fig. 78) are rare, and only occur in England and Wales. It is more likely they were used for hunting large animals than for spearing salmon; and other specimens are shown in Cases A, B, and 9 (Broadward hoard). The long rivet, still in position, is specially connected with this type. Illustrations are here given of American lance or arrow-heads to show the independent invention of the barbed and other forms (fig. 79).

Case E.

There is no doubt that in the Bronze period there was a close connection between the civilisation of France and these islands; and though it is only in Brittany and the Paris basin that close analogies may be looked for, it must be remembered that the Rhone, which belongs rather to the Swiss and Italian areas of culture, was on the highway of early trade between the Mediterranean countries and north-west Europe. The *West* side of the Case is mainly devoted to remains of the neolithic period, discovered in the dolmens of Brittany and the Channel Islands, which cannot be further noticed here. On the *East* side are several typical pieces which serve to mark the stages of the Bronze period in France, as recently defined by Prof. Montelius. Without insisting on the simultaneous development of culture in the two countries, we may give the dates assigned for France as interesting in connection with our own antiquities. The first period, or age of copper, is said to have started some time before 2000 B.C.; and is characterised by pottery, beads, &c., surviving from neolithic times; by daggers of Cypriote type (fig. 117), double-axes recalling stone forms, flat celts, and halbert-blades. The second period (1850–1550) is marked by bronze with about 10 per cent. of tin, in the form of flanged and spoon-shaped celts (fig. 80), rapiers with rounded base, daggers of triangular shape,

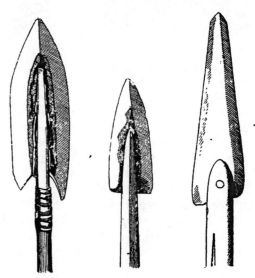

Fig. 78.—Spear-head with rivet, Plaistow, Essex. ¼

Shell and slate, Vancouver Island.

Copper, Arctic America.

Fig. 79.—Forms of lance-heads. ½

simple pins and bracelets with tapering ends. During the transition to the third period appear the socketed spear-head and the celt with stop-ridge; and during that period (1550–1300) cremation is introduced, also tweezers having broad blades, rapiers with two rivet holes and angular base (as Chinon, Indre-et-Loire), bracelets with blunt ends, elaborate pins, the palstave, and the peculiar flanged celt of Italy (fig. 116, Abruzzi). The fourth period (1300–1050) brings celts with wings in the middle and socketed celts, swords with broad tang, chapes sometimes of the

British tapering type, broad and heavy bracelets, razors, and Italian brooches. The fifth period (1050–850) has celts with wings near the butt (fig. 16, no. 2), and socketed examples, of a type common in Britain (fig. 16, no. 3); swords (in the Rhone valley) of a peculiar type occurring in Central Europe (fig. 81), and others with *antennae* (cf. fig. 110); socketed knives, both straight and curved, leaf-shaped swords as in Britain, bracelets with returned ends, trumpet-shaped mounts (as pl. III), and moulded discs like one from the Thames (Case A). The short chape from E. France belongs to this time, and wire bracelets also occur like those from Heneglwys (Case F) and Heathery Burn (p. 85). About the middle of the ninth century the use of iron was learnt from the people of Upper Austria, but as the Hallstatt period is barely represented in Britain by iron objects, our Bronze age no doubt lasted longer. Cremation in the later stages was apparently more uniform on this side of the Channel, as the older rite still continued to be practised in Gaul after the innovation which, according to this chronology, dates from the fourteenth century B.C.

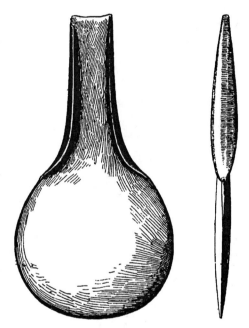

FIG. 80.—Spoon-shaped celt, Aps, Dépt. Ardèche, France. ½

Among the celts should be noticed specimens of types which are confined to certain areas in France and neighbouring countries. The spatula or spoon-shaped celt (fig. 80) is found in the Rhone valley as well as in the Swiss lake-dwellings (Case S) and the terremare of North Italy—another indication that the earliest bronze objects were imported into France across the passes of the Alps or along the Ligurian coast to the neighbourhood of Marseilles. The long socketed celt with a square section at the mouth is practically confined to north-western France, and may be called the Brittany type (fig. 82). There seems to have been a regular export of such celts to the southern coasts of Britain, specimens having been found in Cornwall, Portland, the New Forest, and Sussex.

Another type here represented is the winged celt, which is indeed known in England, but was probably imported in the first instance from France or Germany. It occurs, for example, in the Beachy Head deposit (plate ix), and forms a link in the chain

FIG. 81.—Sword, probably S. France. $\frac{1}{8}$

of development from the flat celt to the socketed variety in this country (p. 41). The notch or opening to be observed in the butt of this and certain other types from France and Italy (p. 117) was due originally to the presence of two projections or jets formed in the runners of the mould and not removed after casting, but hammered over to form a loop. It is difficult to see how this could have been of any service, as the butt was entirely covered by the prongs of the handle (cf. fig. 54).

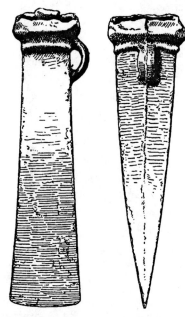

FIG. 82.—Socketed celt, Ergué-Armel, Quimper, Brittany. $\frac{1}{2}$

Other objects of interest are the small anvil (fig. 83), the cylinder with a number of movable rings already referred to (p. 28), and the socketed celt resembling that from Beverley (fig. 65) but with the loop on the face instead of the side (fig. 84). The larger armlet with spiral coils is more common in Hungary (Case G), and the dagger from La Guillotière (fig. 85) is nearer than the Thames specimen (fig. 48) to the original terramara type as seen in Case J. A hollow terminal in the form of a bird from Auvergne resembles one from Hungary (Case G), and, to judge from an analogous example found in Denmark with remains of wood, was probably attached to the end of a chariot-pole. Diminutive socketed celts, the use of which is not apparent, are also exhibited in Case 75.

Case F.

On the *left* of the *East* side are relics from barrows in the northern counties of England, principally from the Greenwell collection. The most interesting and important are the three solid chalk drums (fig. 86), engraved all over with geometrical and

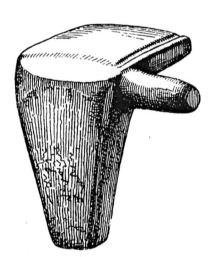

FIG. 83.—Anvil, from the
Rhone district, France. $\frac{2}{3}$

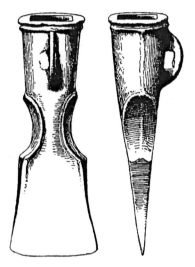

FIG. 84.—Socketed celt, Avignon,
Dépt. Vaucluse France. $\frac{1}{2}$

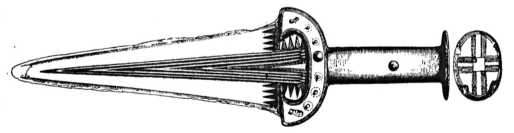

FIG. 85.—Dagger, La Guillotière, Dépt. Rhône, France. $\frac{1}{3}$

other designs, that show connection with the 'Aegean' culture of the Mediterranean. A barrow on Folkton Wold, E. R. Yorks., 54 ft. in diameter, had been reared over a central cairn containing two adult skeletons and a 'drinking-cup'; and round the cairn, at a distance of about 12 ft., a trench had been dug below the original surface. Outside this, about 22 ft. from the centre, another trench had been driven at the same level, but only on the eastern half of the circle. In this trench, east of the central cairn, was the burial containing the chalk drums, while in other parts of the area, on or about the original level, were several other unburnt burials, without any trace of bronze. The relative date of the drums is therefore determined not by their position in the barrow, but by their ornamentation. Both Canon Greenwell and Dr. Arthur Evans draw attention to similar representations of the human face (fig. 87, nos. 1, 3) on early objects from Hissarlik and the Greek Islands; and a small statuette from Pamphylia

FIG. 86.—Chalk drum, Folkton, E. R. Yorks. ⅔

with this feature is shown in Case J. The same motive occurs on the sculptured menhirs (standing stones) of the Marne and Gard valleys in France, while clay vessels with this ornament, belonging to the early age of metal, were found in Spain by the brothers Siret. The 'butterfly' (fig. 87, no. 2) is seen on gold roundels from the earliest (shaft) graves at Mycenae, and the 'double horse-shoe' (fig. 87, no. 1 a) recalls the remarkable sculptures at New Grange, Co. Meath, and Gavr'inis, Brittany. Above all, the degenerate returning spirals (fig. 87, no. 2 a) are a reminiscence of Aegean art, and everything points to the transmission of that influence to the British Isles by way of Spain.

The barrow at Kelleythorpe, Driffield, E. R. Yorks., contained as many as ten burials, but none cremated: with one were found a 'food-vessel' and the bone object exhibited, and this may have been earlier than the cist, which was below the original surface (like fig. 27), and contained a crouching skeleton. On the right wrist was the bracer (bowman's wrist-guard), which was fastened with a strap and small bronze 'buckle,' the latter being found underneath the bones. At the back of the body were the bronze dagger and a 'drinking-cup,' while round the neck had been attached three amber beads, with the under side flat and the

Fig. 87.—Ornamentation of chalk drums, Folkton. ¼

V-shaped perforation characteristic of the early Bronze age in these islands. A mass of linen-cloth lay under the entire length of the skeleton, and was no doubt used as a winding-sheet. This burial is remarkable in more than one particular. Here a 'drinking-cup' is found with bronze (as in a few other cases in Yorkshire) ; the bracer is found in position, though the wearer must have been left-handed, and its gold studs confirm the early date assigned to the remarkable spear-head in Case A.

The small bronze knife from Bradley, Derbyshire. was found in the mouth of a large cinerary urn in Case 18. The stone axe-hammers from Yorkshire (as fig. 93) belong to types that must have survived well into the Bronze age, and are often found with cremated interments in England, though in Scotland they may belong in some cases, as always in Scandinavia, to the neolithic period. Two pieces of pottery are included here as being the

FIG. 88.—'Food-vessel,' Goodmanham, E. R. Yorks.　½

best manufactured and most delicately ornamented met with in the barrows. The bowl (fig. 88) may rank as a 'food-vessel,' and was found in the same barrow as the casket (now restored), which adjoined the cremated remains of a woman. Both are possibly by the same hand, but the bowl may have belonged to a primary unburnt male burial.

To the *right* are ornaments of jet and amber from barrows in various parts of the kingdom. Among several examples of jet buttons with V-shaped perforations should be noticed one of very small bore, found with a bronze celt and skeleton in Soham Fen, Cambs. This specimen, like one from Pen-y-Bonc, Holyhead, was perhaps attached to a necklace like that illustrated from Scotland (fig. 89), which was found with two bronze armlets in a cist containing an unburnt skeleton. Two jet and one bronze ring with lateral perforations, recalling the heavy bronze rings from Ireland (fig. 5), were found, with a razor, at Heneglwys, Anglesey. A remarkably large bead of jet (fig. 90), from a barrow near Bridlington, resembles some found in Ireland, and there can be no doubt that most of the ornaments of that material here shown were made and in use when metal was known. There are unfortunately few details as to the discovery of the large amber necklace in this Case. Sir R. Colt Hoare found it in a barrow at Lake, Wilts., with gold and other ornaments shown in another section, and concluded that it had belonged to a lady of high rank, on whose neck it had been buried.

Among other forms of jet may be mentioned the runner or slide from Hambleton Moor (fig. 91) and the toggles or studs from

FIG. 89.   Jet necklace,   Melfort, Argyllshire.   ⅓

Fylingdales (fig. 92), pro-   bably for fastening the dress
in some way. A flattened jet   ring with pierced projections seems to belong to a   common type of pendant,
and may be compared with   one of 'porcelain' from
Lewes in this section, and   others of bronze from Ex-
ning, Suffolk (Case C), and   France (Case E).

On the *East* side are   objects from barrows in the
south of England, and es-   pecially Wiltshire.   To the
left should be noticed an-   other instance of the sur-
vival of neolithic stone hammers into the Bronze period, a well-formed stone specimen (fig. 93) being found with one of stag's horn (fig. 94) in association with a burnt body in Berkshire. The bracer (fig. 95) from Brandon was found with vessels exhibited in Case 19; and another, with only two holes, was found with a primitive tanged knife and a carved ornament of bone in a grave at Sittingbourne. On a small dagger from Lambourn Down are clear traces of a textile, and an interesting group from Great Shefford in the same county is here shown, including an open 'incense-cup' (fig. 96) and flint scrapers. As exceptional relics from barrows in this country should be noticed the flanged celt from Plumpton, and the socketed spear-head from another barrow near Lewes. The simple bronze cylinders and other beads of glass from the Devil's Dyke, Brighton, were found

on the neck of a skeleton, the grave also containing a 'drinking. cup' (Case 19).

To the *right*, remains from Wiltshire illustrate the peculiar richness of that county. From the same grave as the amber necklace came a pair of gold earrings, and a number of ribbed

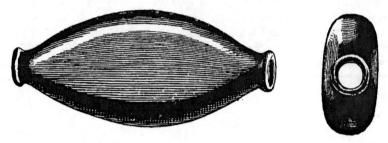

FIG. 90.—Jet bead, Burton Fleming, Bridlington, E. R. Yorks.　⅔

FIG. 91.—Jet slide, Hambleton
Moor, W. R. Yorks.　⅔

FIG. 92.—Jet button, Fylingdales,
Scarborough, N. R. Yorks.　⅔

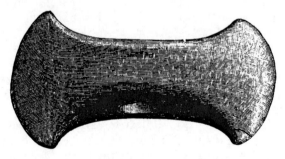

FIG. 93.—Stone axe-hammer, Lambourn Downs, Berks.　½

cylindrical beads (fig. 97), such as occur at Tan Hill and Syrencot Down in the same county, also in Dorset and Cornwall (*left* of Case). They are of glass, but have the appearance of the 'porcelain' common in ancient Egypt, and were no doubt imported. Several bone pins or skewers, probably for pinning the cloak, are shown; but the most interesting objects of this material are four rectangular plates from Lake, one side being convex but both ornamented, and closely resembling those illustrated from Folkton (fig. 37). Some fine examples of the riveted dagger-blade characteristic of the Barrow period, include one with five rivets (fig. 98) from Homington, and another from Syrencot Down clearly show-

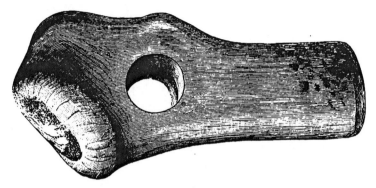

FIG. 94.—Deer-horn hammer, Lambourn Downs, Berks. ½

FIG. 95.—Stone wrist-guard, Brandon, Suffolk. ⅔

ing the outline of the haft at the base of the blade. The edges of these daggers are sometimes curved inwards or outwards, and sometimes practically straight (cf. fig. 126).

GERMANY: Case G.

Germany during the Bronze period was traversed by the two main trade-routes which owed their existence to the wealth of amber on the west coast of Denmark and the South Baltic. The first ran from the head of the Adriatic near Venice up the valley of the Adige, through the Brenner Pass, and down the Inn to Passau, where it joined the Danube. The Bohemian Forest was then crossed to the Moldau, and the North Sea gained by following the Elbe to its mouth. The second route struck off from the Gulf of Trieste, north-east to Laibach, thence to Gratz, and down the

Leitha to the Danube at Pressburg. The tributary March was then ascended, and after crossing Moravia, the route passed through Silesia along the Oder, while the Vistula was reached by striking across Posen, the principal terminus being Dantzic. In connection with the trade-routes it should be mentioned that during the developed period of the Bronze age the spiral, so prevalent in Aegean and Egyptian art, hardly occurs on the Continent west of the Elbe route just described; but as it is clearly seen on the carved stones of the New Grange barrow, Co. Meath, and has been already referred to in connection with the chalk drums from Yorkshire (p. 90), it probably reached the North-west in earlier times by a different route.

FIG. 96.—'Incense-cup,' Great Shefford, Berks. ⅔

Though the Bronze period in Germany has never been systematically treated as a whole, its earliest stage has been considered to be contemporary with the Island (or pre-Mycenaean) culture of the Mediterranean, and to have declined with the Mycenaean, elements of the Hallstatt civilization appearing there at least as soon as 1000 B.C. The early stages are represented over a very wide area, embracing practically all the high ground of Central Europe, from the east of Bohemia to the Middle Rhine and Upper Rhone, while Scandinavia was partially isolated by the flat

FIG. 97.—Glass beads, Tan Hill, Wilts.

country of Northern Germany, where the earliest forms are not so common. Within the larger area the closest connection seems to have been between Bavaria, Würtemberg, Austria, Upper Hungary and Bohemia, identical types of pins and bracelets being found from the last country as far west as the Rhine and Rhone valleys. Southern influences are proved by the presence of a Mediterranean shell (*Columbella rustica*) in graves in Rhenish Hesse and in the basin of the Rhone, and of Egyptian glass beads in South Germany; while at the close of the Bronze age 'cordoned' vessels of North Italian origin were exported into Bohemia as well as into Hungary (p. 117). A sequence of periods similar to that already established for Scandinavia is being formulated for Central Europe, but the forms characteristic of the various stages of development are here neither so numerous nor so universally recognised. Certain types, however, afford important evidence of date ; for example, swords with octagonal hilts seem to belong to a stage corresponding to the second Scandinavian period of Prof. Montelius, while the brooch frequently occurs about the same time, a fact which is held by Prof. Ridgeway and others to refute the commonly accepted derivation of Northern forms from the Mycenaean brooch (p. 124).

To the *left* of the Case, the earliest period of the Bronze age in Germany is well illustrated by the important discovery at Neuenheiligen (Langensalza, Erfurt) in 1776. Part of the find, from the collection of Dr. G. Klemm, of Dresden, is here shown, and includes examples of the flanged celt, of which over sixty were found ; a dagger, possibly of copper and formed by hammering, with the handle in one piece with the blade, resembling a flint dagger ; another dagger of more elaborate form (fig. 99), the grip cast separately ; blades, with part of the shaft, of halberts like the complete one in this Case (fig. 101) ; and a pick (fig. 100) with comparatively small shaft-hole in the centre. In some cases the hole is too

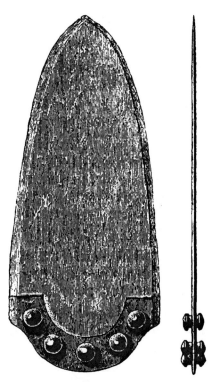

FIG. 98.—Knife-dagger, Homington, Wilts. $\frac{1}{2}$

small to admit even a metal shaft, and it has been suggested that the raw material was imported in this form (somewhat like the iron osmunds of the middle ages), several pieces being held together by a cord passed through the central hole. One specimen with this small perforation has been analysed and found to be of pure copper ; and it is not improbable that more than one piece in the Neuenheiligen find has no tin in its composition. Daggers. like fig. 99 were evidently of local manufacture, based on the Italian terramara types also found in Germany. Another group of the early Bronze age is from Beitzsch, near Pförten, Frankfurt-on-Oder ; the ornamented dagger or halbert-blade serving to date the conical helmet and swelling armlets with rolled ter-

minals of which there are other examples in this Case. Other
objects of the same early date are the remarkable halbert from
Potsdam (fig. 101), the modern appearance of which is partly due
to cleaning ; and a dagger found with a slender celt at Weimar.
It was from celts of this type that the long socketed celt of
Scandinavia was ultimately derived.

   In the series of German celts on the *right*, the winged variety
is predominant, though the palstave without loop as well as

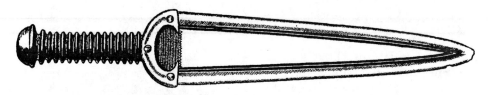

Fig. 99.—Dagger, Neuenheiligen, Langensalza, Erfurt. ⅓

socketed forms occur.   A small group from Camenz, Saxony,
formed part of a hoard which included examples of the celt,
spear, bracelet, torc, and sickle. Of the last there were about
twenty specimens, of two kinds, with a rivet hole and pin respectively for attachment to the handle ; and the celts were all of
the winged variety here exhibited.   A coiled ring of twisted
bronze like one in Case C from Woolmer Forest was also included
in this hoard.   The huge armlets from Kissingen, Bavaria

Fig. 100.—Pick or ingot, Neuenheiligen. ¼

(fig. 102), which are cast hollow and richly ornamented, belong
to the Hallstatt period, which is also represented by a few remains from that famous site near Salzburg in Upper Austria.
Excavations were carried on there between 1847 and 1864, and
over 6,000 objects were obtained from nearly a thousand graves,
just over half of which contained unburnt burials.   Both methods
of interment were contemporary on this site, but it was noticed
that the cremated burials were those of the wealthier class, or
possibly of the dominant race.   The Hallstatt period, however,
belongs rather to the Iron age, and cannot be further treated here,
though certain bronze objects of that period are exhibited in this
Room for the sake of convenience.

HUNGARY.

This country is of exceptional interest, as during the earlier period of the Bronze age its antiquities show many indications of external influence, while the later period witnessed a development of Bronze industry which in splendour and artistic quality is only surpassed by the art of Scandinavia. The part of the Danube valley which lies to the west of the great bend of the river has proved specially rich in primitive remains of metal, for it lay upon the path of early commerce, and the first improvements in industry and art arrived there not very long after their invention. But it is in Transylvania and on the southern slopes of the Carpathians, far from the main routes of intercourse, that the later Bronze civilisation chiefly flourished. Here, in undisturbed seclusion, the more elaborate types and ornaments were developed down to and beyond the time when iron had been introduced into neighbouring countries.

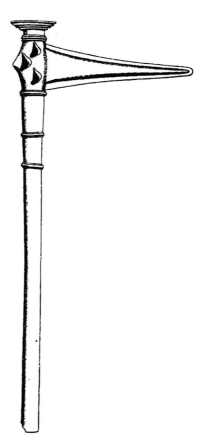

Fig. 101.—Halbert, Trieplatz, Potsdam, Prussia. ⅓

Hungary is remarkable for the great number of its copper implements; and as this metal could be obtained in abundance on the spot, it was natural that it should have been worked at a very early date. It was indeed so abundant that it was exported alike into Northern Europe and into the north-west of Asia Minor, the fact being confirmed by the presence of a certain percentage of nickel characteristic of the Hungarian ores. Some idea of the date when copper was first manufactured into ornaments and implements may be gained from the discoveries in the late neolithic settlement at Lengyel, Tolna. Here beads of almost pure copper were associated with stone implements and pottery vessels with very high feet, one of which was painted with semicircles and spirals in red and yellow. The presence of the spiral indicates Aegean influence, which cannot be earlier than the period between 3000–2500 B.C., when this ornament was first used in the Greek Islands. Within these approximate limits the inhabit-

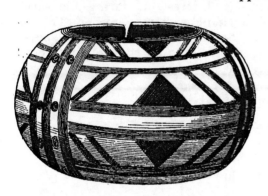

FIG. 102.—Hollow armlet, Kissingen, Bavaria. $\frac{1}{3}$

ants of the Danube valley probably became acquainted with metals, either by independent invention or instruction from a more advanced civilisation. Various evidences of southern and oriental influences seem to favour the second alternative, and among these may be mentioned: daggers of a well-known Cypriote form (fig. 117), presumed to date from the third millennium;

flat axes (*left* of Case), sometimes pierced at the butt, of a type occurring in Greece, the Aegean (fig. 119, *a*), and at Hissarlik; double axes with central shaft-hole and both edges in one

FIG. 103.—Battle-axe, Hungary. $\frac{1}{3}$

FIG. 104.—Sword, Zsujta, Abauj, Hungary. $\frac{1}{6}$

plane, such as are known in Greece (Case J), Cyprus, and Western Asia; axe-adzes with central shaft-hole, also represented by examples from Hissarlik, the Greek Islands (fig. 119, *f*), and Sardinia; spiral gold finger-rings almost identical with rings from the second city of Hissarlik; bronze penannular collars with coiled ends, as known in Italy and Egypt; pins of Cypriote form;

and the pottery vessels from Lengyel, the high feet of which recall certain types from Bohemia, Asia Minor, Spain (fig. 39), and Egypt. Such finds confirm the great antiquity of the Hungarian copper stage of culture, and of the succeeding earliest period of bronze; while the occurrence in a late neolithic cemetery at Lucska, Ungh, of a pierced copper axe-head, is a further proof that there really was a transitional stage in which stone and copper were used together. The introduction of bronze must have taken place very near the beginning of the second millennium.

At that early time Hungary, as has already been stated, formed one of a zone of countries united by a similar Bronze culture stretching from Bohemia to the Middle Rhine and Upper Rhone. The elaborate battle-axes (fig. 103), of which three examples are shown on the *left* of the Case, are characteristic of Hungary, and are attributed by some to a comparatively early period. The existence at Toszeg and elsewhere of terremare related to those of Northern Italy is noticed on p. 113.

The antiquities of the later Hungarian Bronze age show so many similarities to those of Scandinavia, and yet are marked by so many differences, that though both groups must at one time or another have been affected by similar influences, neither can be described as the immediate descendant of the other. It seems probable that this Hungarian industry did not transmit the spiral and other features from south to north, but was rather an isolated local development.

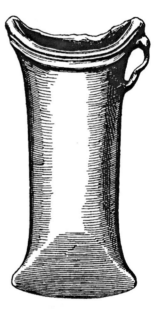

Fig. 105.—Socketed celt, Hungary. ⅔

Most of these later Hungarian finds are not from graves but deposits, in which several objects of the same type, sometimes all undamaged, occur together: thus on one occasion as many as twenty swords were found in one place. Such collections as these must have been either deposited for votive purposes or else concealed as valuable property; but there are also examples of founders' hoards containing 'scrap bronze' destined to be melted down and re-worked; a noted example of the latter was discovered at Hammersdorf in Transylvania. With the swords there have been found imported bronze vessels of types which in Italy and the Eastern Alps belong to the Hallstatt period; the inference being that Eastern Hungary did not use iron until long after the countries further to the south and west. During this later period its culture should be compared with that of the early Iron age as represented at Glasinatz in Bosnia rather than with the older Bronze culture of Northern Europe.

It has been stated that a free employment of spiral ornament is characteristic of the later Hungarian Bronze age. The spirals are frequently coiled from thick bronze wire, often of lozenge or quadrangular section; in this manner are formed the ends of

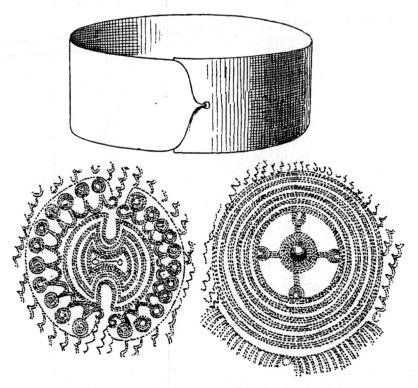

FIG. 106.—Bronze belt, with details, Hungary. ¼ and ⅔

armlets (*left* of Case), torcs and brooches. A peculiarity of Hungarian swords (*right* of Case) is that the broadest part of the blade is nearer the point than the hilt (fig. 104), thus giving the weapon a clumsy and ill-balanced appearance. Some of the celts (*left* of Case) are ornamented with a raised design of straight lines converging on concentric circles; others are sack-shaped (fig. 105). Beyond the limits of the true Bronze period is the broad bronze belt (fig. 106), several examples of which were found in the cemetery at Hallstatt, with very similar ornament executed by means of a finely-pointed punch.

DENMARK: Case H.

Situated at one extremity of the Old World, the Scandinavian countries present certain peculiarities in the neolithic and Bronze ages which are due to their remoteness from the centres of early civilization. They received their culture at a comparatively late date, and in their isolation brought the arts of working stone and bronze to a high degree of perfection, while more advanced nations had already entered the succeeding stage. It must, however, be borne in mind that throughout the Bronze age the amber trade brought merchants, or at least manufactured goods, from the Mediterranean, and fine bronzes evidently of Italian origin are not uncommon in Denmark and South Sweden. It is this proof of early intercourse that has prompted Prof. Montelius, of Stockholm, to regard the Scandinavian Bronze age as dating from the early time when such objects were being produced in Italy, and thus

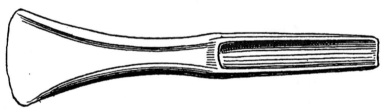

FIG. 107.—Palstave, Denmark. ½

to give it a duration of about thirteen centuries. Another view is taken by Dr. Sophus Müller, of Copenhagen, who does not allow such a rapid transmission of culture in those early times, and places the beginning of the Bronze period in Scandinavia about 1200 B.C., its total duration being about eight centuries, and the division between the early and late stages about 800 B.C. Both these stages are again divided into two parts, and the entire period is thus split up into four sections of about two centuries each. Prof. Montelius' classification is more detailed, and as it is often referred to, may be summarised here. His first period includes the copper implements of rude type which are generally regarded as the earliest metal objects in Europe; while his next four periods extend from the fifteenth or sixteenth century B.C. to the seventh. The Halstatt period of Central Europe is represented in Scandinavia by his sixth (about 650–500 B.C.).

The extreme scarcity of pure tin and copper in the Scandinavian finds of the Bronze age suggests that bronze was at that time imported; and as analysis shows, some came from Central Europe and some from the British Isles, the latter supply being remarkably free from nickel, an alloy which is characteristic of the German ores. Apart from the obvious Italian productions, the manufacture of bronze implements and ornaments was local, and many hoards in Scandinavia, as in England, show moulds, jets, and broken articles ready for remelting. The art of casting bronze was practised with great success in this part of Europe, and the *cire-perdue* process was adopted for bowls, ceremonial axes, and other elaborate productions. There still exist in Sweden and Norway, especially in Bohuslän, Ostgotland, and Scania, a large number of rock-carvings dating from this period, which show that the soil was cultivated, that the horse was used for riding and

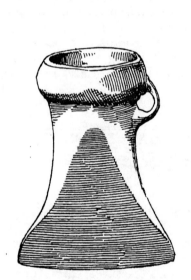

Fig. 108.—Socketed celt, Denmark. ¾

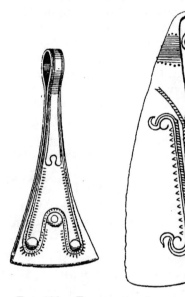

Fig. 109.—Tweezers and razor, Denmark. ¾

driving, that large ships (without sails) were constructed, and that a pictographic script was in existence. Clothing, of which there are considerable remains, was made of skins and wool, but traces of linen are very rare; indeed, implements for spinning and weaving are unaccountably wanting in Scandinavia before the opening of the Iron age. Burial customs roughly correspond to those of England, but the sepulchral pottery differs. In the first part of the Bronze age the dead were buried unburnt in stone cists or in tree-trunks split and hollowed for the purpose. Later on, the bodies were burned, and the ashes preserved in small stone cists or in simple urns of pottery. The graves were generally covered with a barrow or cairn, and in many cases the central and primary grave is a cist, while other later interments have been made in the mound (cf. figs. 27, 28). Three parts of this Case contain antiquities from Denmark, chiefly from the collections of Dr. Worsaae and Capt. A. P. Madsen.

On the *West* side, to the *left*, are arranged a number of celts in their probable chronological sequence: special attention may be drawn to the long narrow palstaves without loops (fig. 107) and the small socketed celts with triangular faces (fig. 108), both being

FIG. 110.—Sword with ' antennae,' Denmark. ⅛

types most common in Scandinavia. A variety of razors and tweezers (fig. 109), knives and pins, are shown, and ships occur on several of the razors as an ornamental feature. The bronze jug has no history, but is most probably from Denmark, and dates from the later Bronze age; while the bronze box beside it, with a scroll design on the base, belongs to the fifth period of Prof. Montelius, and forms the last link in the chain of development

FIG. 111.—' Spectacle' brooch, Denmark. ⅔

established for these caskets. A fragment of an earlier form, with pointed base, has traces of the clay which formed the inner mould, the interstice having originally been filled by a wax model.

To the *right* are weapons, some of which are highly ornamented, one short sword having gold plates attached to the edges of the grip. The swords are for the most part earlier than those in this country, and have complete metal grips, while the blade is not ordinarily leaf-shaped, but straight or tapering. Those with the handle in one piece with the blade but with flanged edges only (cf. pl. VIII) are comparatively late, while the perfect specimen of the *antennae* type (fig. 110) belongs to the Hallstatt period.

On the *East* side, to the *left*, are torcs and ornaments, the former including a triple example resembling that illustrated from Portugal (fig. 142), though without the calyx-shaped projec-

tions. Of the torcs or twisted collars, one type has expanding
ends with terminals of coiled wire, another has rectangular
catches.   The smallest brooch of the four grouped together is
nearest the prototype, which resembled a modern safety-pin ; and
the wire coils at the end may still be traced in the enlarged and
flattened ends of the two belonging to the fourth period (fig. 111).
A portion of a trumpet with raised spiral ornament retains the
mouthpiece and several loops near it, from which originally hung
short chains and metal clappers.

RUSSIA AND SIBERIA : FURTHER ASIA.

The bronze antiquities discovered in the north of Russia, in
Finland and the Baltic Provinces, are closely related to those of
Scandinavia and Northern Germany, and belong to the same
archaeological region ; but in the south of the country we find
traces of two distinct groups.   In the basin of the Volga and
beyond it to the Dnieper there is a western extension of the Ural-
Altaic province ; and about the lower Dnieper, especially in the
Governments of Kieff and Ekaterinoslav, a Bronze culture more
akin to that of Central Europe.   Among the products of this
latter industry are tanged and socketed spear-heads, flat and
socketed celts, sickle-like knives, daggers, arrow-heads, and personal
ornaments such as bracelets ; and some of these objects are stated
to be of pure copper.   The remarkable pottery discovered in the
Ukraine, on the site of prehistoric settlements, is ascribed by
Russian archaeologists to the transition between the neolithic and
Bronze periods.   It is ornamented with incised and painted curvi-
linear or scroll designs, which, in conjunction with the spirals on
certain bronze ornaments and the occurrence of small earthenware
statuettes, have suggested a connection with the products of the
early Aegean culture preceding the Mycenaean age.   There is
certainly a marked similarity between some of the incised pottery
and the ruder ware from the neolithic station at Butmir in Bosnia,
where the occurrence of pottery with spiral designs of the finest
execution, and statuettes of pronounced Aegean type, place an
early Mediterranean influence beyond question ; and pottery discovered in Thrace and Thessaly is in many respects analogous. To
the north of the Caucasus, in Daghestan, Kabarda, and Abkhasia,
remains of the Bronze age have been found, perhaps indicating,
like the dolmens of the same region, a very early communication
with Asia.
The problem presented by the antiquities of south-eastern
Russia and Siberia is one of considerable difficulty.   At both

extremities of the vast area stretching from Lake Baikal through the southern Siberian steppes across the Ural Mountains to the basin of the Volga, and even beyond to the valleys of the Don and Dnieper, there have been found, generally in tombs but occasionally on the surface of the ground, implements and weapons marked by the same peculiarities of form and by a single style of decoration. These objects exhibit an undoubted affinity with those discovered in China ; but some of their distinctive features have been traced in the Bronze industry of Hungary and the Caucasus: for example, pierced axes and sickles have a close resemblance to Hungarian and Caucasian forms. The Siberian bronzes have thus relationships both in the East and West ; but their kinship with Chinese antiquities being the more obvious, it is natural to assume that the culture which they represent is of East Asiatic origin. The presumable antiquity of Chinese civilisation ; the continued westward tendency of migrations in historical times ; the later and more developed character which has been remarked in the objects from the European extremity of this Ural-Altaic province ; and the fact that the greatest centre of discovery lies far away to the East in the basin of the Yenisei, in the districts of Minusinsk and Krasnoiarsk ; are all points which may be urged in support of this view. There are, however, facts which this hypothesis does not completely explain. Most of the known Chinese bronze implements are of developed and therefore not of primitive forms, such as socketed celts and spear-heads, picks with animal ornament in the round, knives and daggers with decorative handles cast in one piece with the blade, horse-bits, and large bronze vessels. Such forms can only have been reached after a long period of evolution, but their prototypes are found neither in the Ural-Altaic region itself, where some objects may indeed be simpler in design than others but cannot be described as quite primitive ; nor as yet within the limits of China, at any rate not in sufficient number or variety to establish a true descent. But it must be remembered that the prehistoric archaeology of China is still in its infancy, and that we know but a trifling percentage of the remains which the soil of that country conceals. Socketed celts found in Yunnan and Cambodia have been compared with Siberian forms, and points of resemblance have been noted in halberts (fig. 112), shafted axes, daggers and swords from various parts of China (**Case K**) : future discoveries will certainly add to the list, and may throw an important light upon the early cultural relations in south-east Asia, which, it may be remembered, is a district rich both in copper and tin. Although the evidence on which their conclusions are based may not stand the test of scientific criticism, the Chinese themselves certainly ascribe a high antiquity to their early bronze weapons. An inscription on the box containing an axe in Case K states that the axe was made under the Chang dynasty (between the years

1766–1122 B.C.), the earlier part of the period to which the so-called classical bronzes are ascribed by native writers.   Another axe in the same Case has an inscription to the effect that it was made in the time of the Chou dynasty; a very similar inscription in the Po Ku Tu mentions Prince P'ing Wang of the same dynasty, and is of the eighth century B.C.; but it is doubtful whether this axe can really be of so early a date.   One thing is clear, that the number of Chinese implements at present known is large enough to prove the existence of a Bronze age in the Far East against those Orientalists who formerly denied it; yet it is difficult

FIG. 112.—Halbert-blade, China.   ½

to say how long an exclusively Bronze culture lasted, as there appears to be still a difference of opinion as to the respective dates at which bronze and iron were first used.   The latter metal was certainly introduced very late into the remoter parts of the Southern Provinces of Kwang-tung and Kwang-Si, for when in the first century A.D. the famous Chinese general Ma defeated the Man, or early inhabitants of these regions, he seized an enormous number of bronze weapons still employed by his opponents, and melted them down to make boundary columns, trophies, and large metal drums.   The socketed spear-head exhibited in Case K, dating, according to the inscription upon it, from the year 209 A.D., unless made for ceremonial use, would also seem to show that bronze weapons were still made in China much later than they were in Europe.   The bronze implements, socketed celts, &c., found in Burma, Java, and Celebes belong to the Southern-Chinese and Annamite archaeological province.   The Japanese also acquired the art of metal-working from China, and when they passed from the mainland into the islands occupied by the stone-using Ainu, were already in their late Bronze age.   The bronze swords discovered, more especially in Kyūshū, had ceased to be used at the time when the Japanese dolmens were constructed, that is to say, in the period closing about the seventh century A.D. China having thus maintained a civilisation based on the use of bronze from a remote period, and transmitted it beyond its own borders towards the north-east, may well have spread the same culture in the opposite direction; and it has been suggested that through the pressure of invasion or over-population a people in possession of the Chinese Bronze culture may have been driven to seek a new home in the Yenisei valley, where they would be free to develop their industry undisturbed during the course of several centuries.

The similarities existing between the Far Eastern and Hungarian groups will not be fully explained until the Bronze age of Southern Asia as a whole is far better known than it is at present. According to a view which has found some acceptance, the common elements may have been derived from some centre in southern or south-western Asia, from which issued two streams of influence, one passing to the north of the Caucasus. the other to China by a southerly route.

Reverting to the Siberian group, which is represented by an enormous number of specimens in the Minu-sinsk Museum, we may notice in a few words the conditions under which discoveries have been made. The

FIG. 113.—Socketed celt, Kertch, S. Russia. ⅔

tombs are rectangular and surrounded by upright slabs of stone, among which are occasionally found rude statues of men and women. On some of these stones and statues are engraved alphabetic characters, as yet undeciphered, which have been compared with the runes of Northern Europe, and similar statues are found as far west as Southern Russia, where they are known as *Kamenniya Babi*, ' old women of stone.' Each grave generally contained several bodies, apparently once covered with wooden slabs or enclosed in stone cists, and above these were bones of animals, especially of horses and sheep; coarse grey pottery, usually broken, and bronze implements were placed with the bodies. The principal classes of bronze antiquities discovered are socketed celts, some with two loops (fig. 113), straight daggers, knives with a single edge (fig. 114, *b*), sickles, picks, pierced axe-heads, socketed spear and arrow-heads, chisels, gouges, pins, bits for horses, circular mirrors, plaques in

the shape of reindeer and other animals, probably used as ornaments to leather girdles, and bronze bowls, usually on high feet.
The most characteristic ornament represents animals of local
species, bears, reindeer, wild goats, &c., the monsters characteristic
of the later Iron age tombs being absent.   Sometimes the heads
of animals are placed back to back so as to form the guards of

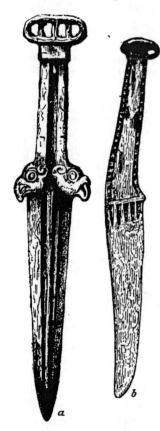

daggers (fig. 114, *a*), a disposition which
has some resemblance to that of daggers
ɪepresented upon Assyrian monuments.
Ancient copper mines are found throughout the region, both in the Altai and
Sajansk Mountains and in the Ural
range ; and the evidence of moulds and
crucibles shows that implements were
manufactured on the spot.

From the fertile nature of sites selected for settlement, the discovery of
irrigation channels, the great number of
sickles, and from the comparative rarity
of horse furniture, it is concluded that
the first metal-using people of the Yenisei
were not nomadic but agricultural. The
apparent absence of neolithic remains
would indicate that these regions were
unoccupied before the introduction of
metal.

A comparison of objects from the
transitional cemetery of Ananino on
the Kama with remains from Graeco-
Scythian tombs in Southern Russia would
seem to show that on the European side
this Ural-Altaic Bronze culture came to
an end about the third century B. C.   The
absence in early Chinese records of any
mention of bronze-using tribes amongst
the peoples of Central Asia perhaps
points to a similar date for the eastern

FIG. 114.—Bronze knives,
Siberia. ⅓

extremity of the line.   Herodotus states that the Massagetae, who
occupied a part of the intervening territory, were still using bronze
in the sixth century B. C.

A word may be added here on the Bronze industry of ancient
Mexico and Peru, which some have endeavoured to connect with
that of China. The independent invention of an alloy like bronze
is indeed not out of the question, and the balance of authority
is now in favour of it, so great are the difficulties in demonstrating
any connection between the bronze implements of the old and
new continents. Most students of American archaeology are

agreed that the Mexican and Peruvian bronzes are not of any very great antiquity, and that the Bronze age must have been over in China long before it began in the New World. Moreover, up to the present time no remains have been discovered south of the Behring Strait on the Asiatic side which might establish a connecting link. Examples of bronze axes, &c., from Mexico and Peru, may be seen in the American Room.

ITALY AND SICILY: Case J.

It is probable that metal was known earliest in the south and centre of the Italian peninsula, but in the north there are remains of extreme antiquity. At Remedello, near Brescia, a cemetery of more than 300 graves was discovered, which clearly extends over a very long period, the celts exhibiting a development from the most primitive types imitating those of stone, to more advanced forms with flanges and expanding edges. These, like the primitive daggers from the same site, are all of copper; and as at Santa Cristina, also in the province of Brescia, a flat copper celt was found with one of the beakers characteristic of the transitional period between stone and metal (p. 54), it may be fairly concluded that Italy passed through a copper stage before proceeding to the use of bronze. In the province of Syracuse in Sicily, Professor Orsi has also discovered graves of the late Stone and transitional periods. At Stentinello there was a settlement which yielded stone implements together with the incised pottery inlaid with a white chalky substance which characterises the transition in several European countries; and pottery of a similar character was found at Villafrate, south-east of Palermo, with a beaker, which probably carries the date back beyond 2500 B.C. It cannot be stated with absolute certainty that metal was known on these early Sicilian sites, for metal objects are not yet forthcoming; but as copper appears with similar pottery in Sardinia, it is very probable that the same was the case in the larger and more easterly island. The early Bronze age in Sicily is represented in the provinces of Syracuse, Girgenti, and Palermo by round tombs hollowed out of the ground, and containing flat axes with painted pottery of indigenous character. The ornament upon this ware resembles that upon early Cypriote vases, while many of the forms recall those of the second city of Troy. A connection with Hissarlik is also suggested by the practical identity of certain curiously decorated objects of bone from that site with those found at Castelluccio and other places in the province of Syracuse: an oriental influence is also indicated by the form of the graves. According to Professor Montelius, the coincidences above indicated place the earliest Bronze period in Sicily between 2500 and 2000 B.C.: the earlier Copper period, with remains of which the beakers occur, should therefore date from the middle or the earlier half of the third millennium.

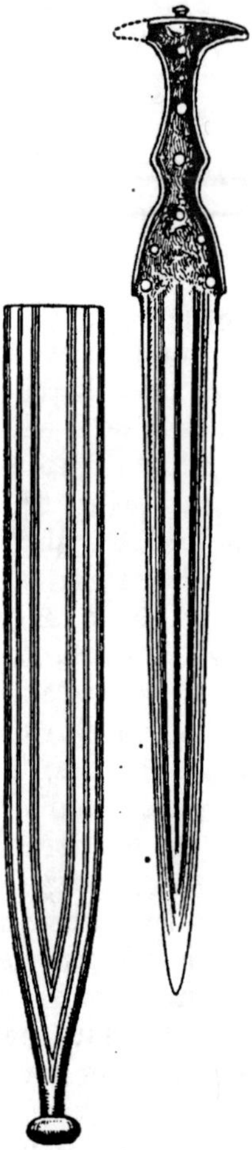

Both Sicily and Italy have yielded remains of the fully developed 'Mycenaean' Bronze culture. In Sicily these remains are situated in the neighbourhood of Syracuse (Plemmirio, il Fusco, Cozzo del Pantano, Thapsos, Pantalica), as well as in the neighbourhood of Girgenti and elsewhere. The cemeteries are composed of round graves similar in form to those of the early Bronze age, but larger, and have yielded Mycenaean swords and brooches. The occurrence of these brooches is important, as they are of a more developed form than the Peschiera type from North Italy, and therefore suggest that this last is earlier than the latest phase of the Mycenaean period (p. 124). In Southern Italy, at Cumae and the neighbourhood, swords of a derivative Mycenaean form have been found, while Central Italy itself developed a type of sword the prototype of which has been discovered at Corinth: all these weapons date from about the beginning of the first millennium B.C., and to this period must also belong the dagger with bronze scabbard here illustrated (fig. 115). The influence of the Mycenaean culture spread up the eastern coast as far as the head of the Adriatic, whence it was ultimately diffused to the north and west of the Alps; we have already seen that Aegean influences had passed up the Adriatic at a far earlier period.

FIG. 115.—Dagger with scabbard, Italy. ¼

The conditions under which the Bronze industry was introduced into and developed in Northern Italy are distinct from those which prevailed in the South. In the great northern plains the Bronze age is chiefly represented by the *terremare*, which must now be briefly described. The general aspect of the Po Valley in prehistoric times was very different from that which characterises an Italian landscape to-day. The familiar myrtles and olives, the cypresses, laurels, and evergreen trees did not then exist; the great alluvial plain was not, as now, an open expanse cultivated to the last acre, but was covered by an almost continuous forest of oaks, elms, and other deciduous trees. Through this densely wooded tract flowed the Po and its affluents, and it was near their banks, or on the shores of the lakes, that the earliest habitations were situated.

The distinguishing feature common to all these dwellings was their elevation upon piles, and they may be divided into two main classes: lake-dwellings proper built over water, and the terremare situated upon dry land, the second class being very probably a derivative of the first. The lake-dwellings proper are found in the shallow water near the shores of the Lombard lakes, usually those of small size, or in peat-bogs which have formed over what were once shallow sheets of water. They are similar in character to the settlements in Switzerland, Bavaria, and Austria, and the remains brought to light by excavation testify to a general similarity in the culture of these countries (p. 96). The relics which have been found in the Italian lakes include stone implements as well as bronze, and in some sites, as in those of Lake Varese, east of Lake Maggiore, the former predominate ; but other sites — for example, the great settlement at Peschiera on the southern shore of the Lake of Garda—appear to belong exclusively to the age of Bronze. The lake-dwellings were probably founded either at the end of the Stone age or at the very beginning of the Bronze period, when implements of stone still remained for a considerable time in common use ; and before the close of that period their occupation in most cases came to an end. The occurrence at the higher levels in the peat-bogs of objects belonging to later epochs shows that some sites were occupied in the early Iron age, and even in Roman times, but it is to the Bronze age that the greatest extension of pile structures must be attributed.

The principal objects found in the lakes consist of stone hammers, stone axes and chisels, chipped flint saws, arrowheads and scrapers, numerous implements and utensils of wood, flanged and winged bronze axes, bronze daggers with holes for rivets, socketed spear-heads, knives, two-edged razors, and pins. Bone and earthenware spindle-whorls are common, and there is a great variety of hand-made pottery with incised or impressed geometrical ornament. The ware is of two kinds: a fine, almost black, and a coarser, grey or reddish ; and many vessels are provided with pierced projections for suspension. Long swords do not occur, and the rare brooches are of simple forms, the earliest of which, probably dating from about the fourteenth century B. C., has been named the Peschiera type from the site of its discovery in the settlement at the south end of the Lake of Garda. For the relationship of this type to that found at Mycenae, and that occurring in Sicily, see pp. 124 and 112.

The terremare receive their name from *terra marna* or marl earth, a phrase used by the peasants of Parma, who were in the habit of carting away the rich soil formed by these prehistoric deposits as a fertiliser for their fields.   They are low oblong mounds, usually several acres in extent, and are found in considerable numbers both north and south of the Po in the provinces of Lombardy and Emilia.   In most cases they rise above the level of the surrounding country, but sometimes the accumulation of alluvial soil brought down by the Po and its tributaries has completely concealed them from view.   The terramara settlement began as an enclosed village on level ground surrounded by an earth rampart.   The interior was occupied by rows of circular thatched huts, probably with wattle and daub walls and plank floors, built on piles some six to nine feet in height.   As it seems to have been the custom for the inhabitants to allow all refuse to accumulate in the spaces between the piles, where it was doubtless often covered with mud deposited by river floods, the ground level was constantly rising, so that it often became necessary to re-erect the houses on fresh piles and increase the height of the rampart.   In this manner it is possible to explain the existence of the superimposed settlements found on many of these sites, and to account for the height of many of the mounds above the surrounding plain.   Traces of conflagration have frequently been met with, and it has been conjectured that when reconstruction had to be undertaken, villages were deliberately burned down to make way for the new ones to be built above them ; but the chance fires which must frequently have occurred in settlements formed of inflammable materials may well account for many of these instances.   The *terra marna*, the rich soil so much in request for agricultural purposes, is that formed by the successive accumulations of *débris,* and consists of narrow undulating layers of variously coloured earths : it is these strata which have yielded the greater part of the antiquities discovered during the series of systematic explorations carried out since the year 1861 by Strobel, Gastaldi, Chierici, Pigorini and other Italian archaeologists.   Special mention may be made of the terramara Castellazzo (Fontanellato in the province of Parma), which was surrounded by a ditch filled with running water, and divided into four quarters by two streets cutting each other at right angles.   Within the enclosure on the east side was a rectangular terrace, also surrounded by water, and probably serving a religious purpose ; while at two points beyond the outer ditch were rectangular cemeteries, one similarly enclosed, the ashes being placed in urns on platforms supported by small piles, so that the last resting-places of the dead resembled their homes during life.   Near one of these cemetries was a burning ground, where the bodies had been consumed by fire.

It may at first sight appear strange that the people of the terremare should have taken the trouble to build pile-dwellings when they did not live in lakes or marshes; but they probably adopted the custom when they lived further north as lake or marsh-dwellers in the stricter sense of the term, and may have continued the old method of construction partly from a spirit of conservatism, partly from the necessity for keeping the floors dry in a situation frequently damp and sometimes inundated. It may be recalled that houses built on piles over dry land are no uncommon thing in the modern savage world, especially in the Malay area, and that the sense of security is increased by living at this elevation whether the settlement is surrounded by water or not.

As in the case of the Italian lake-dwellings, to which they have a close cultural relation, the terremare contain remains both of stone and bronze — stone implements being most numerous in the settlements of Lombardy, and bronze predominating in the province of Emilia south of the Po. The types resemble those already described from the lakes, the flat type with flanges or wings being the prevalent form of bronze axe, while swords are extremely rare. The pottery is also similar to that of the lakes, the most characteristic type of the terremare having handles terminating above in two horn-like projections, a peculiarity which occurs in a more rudimentary form in the lake-dwellings in and near the Lake of Garda. Ornament is purely geometric and chiefly confined to such figures as triangles and concentric circles. Daggers with triangular blades (like fig. 85) are frequent enough to be described as the terramara type, and these weapons, from which the simplest form of sword was soon developed, are considered to date from about 2000 B.C. The brooch came in towards the end of the terramara period in the second half of the second millennium: it was of a simple form like the Peschiera type mentioned above (p. 113).

The inhabitants of the terremare were agricultural, raising crops of wheat, barley, millet, beans, and flax; planting the vine, though probably unable to make wine; and keeping cattle, sheep, pigs, goats, dogs, and horses. They wove garments of flax, and were able to work their own metal, as is proved by the occurrence of moulds in which implements were cast.

The discovery in Hungary, notably at Toszeg in the valley of the Theiss, of similar structures first founded in the Stone age, has been taken to indicate that the terramara civilization came into Italy from the basin of the Danube by the passes of the Julian Alps. The historical allusions to the existence of pile-dwellings in the Balkan peninsula and on the Phasis (p. 135) would seem to show that this form of habitation was once widespread in countries lying further to the east. Tombs with both burnt and unburnt remains, containing bronze swords and other objects, are also known in Northern Italy.

It may not be amiss to notice in this connection the influence which Italy exerted on the countries to the north during the Bronze age. It has been commonly held that the Alps were an insuperable barrier, cutting off the peoples to north and south

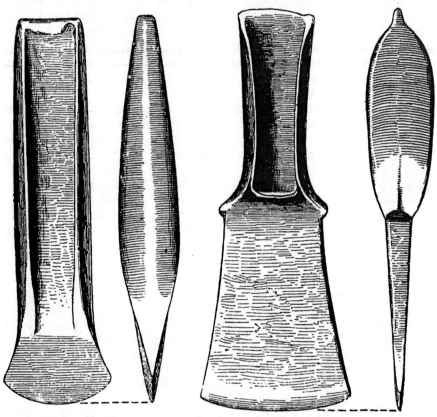

The Abruzzi.   Fiesole, Florence.
FIG. 116.—Flanged celt and palstave, Italy. ½

from rapid communication with each other. But Professor Montelius contests this view, drawing attention to the regular intercourse along the amber route (p. 95), down the Moldau and the Elbe, which he considers to have existed as far back as the third millennium B.C. He points out that imported bronze daggers of the terramara type are found in North Germany, and local imitations of them both in Germany and Scandinavia. In the middle of the second millennium bronze cups, brooches, and spiral ornaments of southern origin are common in the North, while not much later than 1000 B.C. bronze swords of a type frequent in Central

Europe and Italy are found in Denmark and Scandinavia. From about the same time date bronze vessels ornamented with rude copies of the sun's disc between two *uraeus* snakes, which can be traced from Denmark through North Germany and Bohemia to North and Central Italy, where they were evidently manufactured. Similar proofs of continuous commercial relations can be traced down to Roman times; and as the sequence of forms is from first to last the same on both sides of the Alps, while the changes of style are numerous and rapid, northern imitations were almost contemporaneous. It has been stated above that some other Scandinavian archaeologists are not in agreement with these views (p. 103).

The *West* side of Case J is devoted to Italy, and to the *left* are arranged a number of celts, the earliest in the top row, and those with horned butts (p. 88) in the middle. The most primitive form (Abruzzi and Capua) closely resembles the Butterwick specimen (fig. 33), and the heavy flanged type (fig. 116, Abruzzi) is common in the Alpine district. The shouldered type in the third row (fig. 116, Fiesole) occurs at Villanova and Hallstatt, and belongs to the Iron age, which in Italy began early, about 1000 B.C.

On the *right* are spear-heads, some with facetted sockets (cf. fig. 136), and small holes in the base of the blades; razors, such as occur in the terremare and lake-dwellings; and daggers of the terramara type (cf. fig. 85), which was introduced into the countries to the north. A halbert-blade, said to have been found at Calvatone, Cremona, bears a striking resemblance to Irish specimens (fig. 60).

THE EASTERN MEDITERRANEAN.

The Aegean Sea forms the centre of a wide archaeological province, and the influence of its early culture was not confined to Crete, Cyprus, Greece, the Greek Islands and Anatolia, but was felt far into the centre of Europe. Egypt, which had known bronze since the fourth millennium B.C., was at a very early time in communication with the Islands, and to the discoveries which prove this intercourse we owe the most valuable evidence as to the date of primitive metal culture in the Eastern Mediterranean. Thus, scarabs of the twelfth dynasty occur at Hagios Onuphrios in Crete, with pottery similar to that of Amorgos and of the second city at Hissarlik; and Cretan pottery of the Kamáres type comes from the twelfth-dynasty site of Kahun in Egypt. We are therefore justified in assuming that this early Aegean culture was flourishing from before 2500 B.C. to approximately 2000 B.C., after which date it merged into the developed Bronze age civilisation to which the distinctive name 'Mycenaean' has been given (p. 123). It is clear that throughout this early period products of the more advanced countries in and around the Aegean travelled for very great distances ; cultural influences connect Switzerland, Bohemia, various parts of Austria-Hungary, and the Lower Danube with Hissarlik, Cyprus and the Cyclades ; while the coast of Spain has yielded remains in many respects analogous to those of the earlier settlements of Troy (p. 134). The extent to which even remoter parts of Europe were gradually affected by such influences is well illustrated by the distribution of the spiral ornament. Starting in Ancient Egypt, where it was a common form of scarab decoration under the twelfth dynasty, it first reached Crete some time before 2000 B.C., and was especially employed in the decoration of steatite seals ; from Crete it spread to the Islands and the mainland, where it is found on neolithic pottery at the pile-station of Butmir in Bosnia ; thence it followed the amber route along the Moldau and Elbe to the North Sea shores of Jutland, and thus found early entry into Scandinavia. Nor is this all, for either by this or a more southerly route by the islands of the West Mediterranean, Spain, and France, it penetrated to the British Isles quite early in the Bronze age (p. 90). In east Central Europe it is found beyond the Carpathians in the south-west of Russia (p. 106).

All over the area in question, with the apparent exception of Cyprus, where stone implements are exceedingly rare, the culture based on the use of metals was preceded by an earlier neolithic civilisation, which in Crete ended before 3000 B.C.; and in some parts, at least, the first step towards metallurgical knowledge was the working of unalloyed copper ores. In Egypt, as well as Cyprus and Mesopotamia, the arguments for a Copper stage are convincing ; but at Hissarlik the old conclusions in favour of a Copper stage in the lowest strata have been rendered more uncertain by the most recent work on the Schliemann Collection at Berlin. It would now appear that most of the metal types formerly assigned to the first settlement are equally characteristic of higher strata ; and as some confusion of objects found in different levels at the time of excavation was unavoidable, it cannot be confidently stated that they are coeval with the first settlement ; the most that can be said is that the two knives ("Ilios" Nos. 118 and 119) may possibly be of that age, as they differ somewhat from later examples. It should further be noted that in 1893 a *bronze* pin was discovered apparently with just as high claims to a first-settlement origin ; while it is now proved that flat celts with a very low percentage of tin and in all respects resembling those of the second settlement have been found in the sixth stratum (the Homeric Troy), which is approximately dated

1500–1000 B. C. Little therefore on this site points to a gradual increase in the percentage of tin in the bronze (p. 7). On the contrary, the analyses of metal objects from the second settlement, which is supposed to have begun about 2500 B. C., reveal a percentage of from 8–11 per cent. of tin, and thus show that the culture of this city was that of a Bronze and not a Copper age. It may be noted in passing that a tongue-shaped bar of iron very similar to certain silver ingots, which undoubtedly belong to the second settlement, has been claimed as of similar date. There is nothing unreasonable in the claim, for iron has occurred in Egypt as early as the fourth dynasty (p. 2), and was worked in Syria at a very early time. The bronze weapons and implements found in the second to the fifth settlements at Hissarlik (about 2500–1500 B. C.), which include the pre-Mycenaean period in the Aegean, consist of tanged daggers, long flat celts running almost to a point at the butt, knives, razors, saws, and vessels with handles. Gold and silver vessels and beakers occur, and there is much jewellery in the form of earrings, pins, bangles, &c., of the precious metals. Neither the sword nor the brooch was known, and stone axes and axe-hammers were in use throughout. Very characteristic of this early period are small stone (usually marble) idols, sometimes mere pebbles, so formless or so highly conventionalised that their real nature is not at first sight obvious: only in comparatively few instances are eyes, nose, and hair roughly indicated by incised marks. Such 'idols' or amulets are also common in the Cyclades, where, however, the figures are often realistic; they occur in Cyprus, and have even been found in Spain. Other examples, more or less conventionally treated, were made of pottery, and one from Adalia of the late neolithic or earliest Bronze period, with characteristic 'owl-face' and incised ornament filled with chalk, is exhibited in Case J ; but perhaps the earliest examples known are from the neolithic settlement at Hagios Onuphrios in Crete, which cannot be later than 3000 B. C. It has been conjectured, though with little probability, that these idols were primarily derived from clay figures of a Babylonian Mother-goddess, examples of which, of uncertain date, have been found at Nippur. Rude truncated clay female figures from the pile-settlements of Laibach in Carniola are considered to show a relationship with these early amulets of the Aegean, and the same may perhaps be said of others found in the Ukraine (p. 106). Into the complicated question of the development of pottery in pre-Mycenaean Hissarlik it is impossible here to enter; but it may be noted that the use of the potter's wheel and the covered furnace came in during the second settlement, and therefore presumably before 2000 B. C.; and mention may be incidentally made of the well-known pots on which features and limbs are conventionally modelled, the whole vessels being intended to represent a human figure. Vessels with pierced loops for suspension, jugs, beakers with and without handles, shallow bowls, and pottery imitating animal forms, are among the more prominent types. The ornament consists of simple incised geometrical patterns which in the first settlements are inlaid with white earth; the spiral appears at the close of the period, the most characteristic pottery being covered with a red slip and mechanically polished.

The pre-Mycenaean antiquities of **Cyprus** are found both in settlements and tombs in the eastern half of the island, and usually in the neighbourhood of river valleys. The cemeteries are of great extent, and burial was universal, cremation being evidently unknown. Pottery was made on the wheel only at the end of the period, and the ware, either left in the natural colour or converted by firing into red or black, was polished by burnishing; the similarity of technique suggests a comparison with the pre-dynastic Egyptian pottery discovered at Ballas and Naqada, but there is more evident affinity with the early wares of Hissarlik. Many of the Cypriote vessels seem to derive their forms from the gourd-vessels, the use of which has survived in the island to the present day. Ornament was at first chiefly confined to incised geometrical patterns, but in the latter part of the period designs were painted dull white. A black punctuated ware which is found in Cypriote tombs with copper objects has occurred in Egypt on twelfth-dynasty sites (2450–2250 B.C.).

The implements and weapons are flat celts and daggers with rivets or tangs (fig. 117), made at first of copper, or bronze with very little tin; arrow-heads are absent, and spear-heads, if exis-

Fig. 117.—Copper tent, are hardly distinguishable from daggers. dagger, Cyprus. ¼ Small objects like pins, awls, rings, bracelets, and other ornaments are usually of bronze, but the brooch does not occur among them. Cyprus, owing to its wealth of copper, was like Hungary and the Sinaitic peninsula a very early centre of metal-working, but whether the copper industry of Central Europe was independent of Cyprus or not is a matter still disputed by archaeologists of different schools. It is certain that Cypriote forms (daggers) occur in Central Europe (local specimens exist in the museums at Buda-Pesth and Berne), while the inlaying of incised designs with white earth is found at Hissarlik, in Austrian and Swiss lake-dwellings, and in a still ruder style in barrow pottery in Britain. Cyprus did not supply

Egypt with copper until a later period, for, as has been noted elsewhere, Mount Sinai was the earliest source from which Egyptian copper was derived. Nor did it suggest the forms of Egyptian implements, which were indigenous. But Cypriote copper weapons were exported into Egypt, though not in great numbers. Whether the initiative belongs to the East or to Europe, there were undoubtedly relations between the Danubian Valley and the Balkan Peninsula, Asia Minor and Cyprus, at this early period, and Hissarlik as a kind of half-way house was influenced from both sides.

The pre-Mycenaean antiquities of the **Cyclades** have been partly obtained from shallow, rectangular cist-graves, lined with stone slabs, in which the bodies were placed in a squatting position. These antiquities, which cover the long period preceding the fifth settlement at Hissarlik, consist of daggers, tanged spear-heads and flat celts, said to be chiefly of copper. With them are found stone and obsidian implements and flakes, which evidently still remained in use, cup-like vessels cut from the solid marble, and curious stone idols in the form of human figures, already mentioned, some of which assume quite conventional forms, one type resembling a violin: silver occurs in the tombs, but not gold.

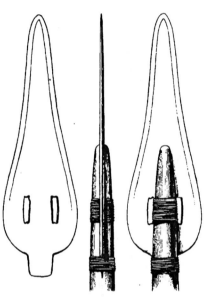

FIG. 118.—Spear-head, Amorgos, with method of hafting. ⅓

Pottery was plentiful, but most of it was made without the wheel, and decorated with incised designs, and, at the end of the period, with painted geometrical ornament and spirals, the latter possibly transmitted from **Crete**. This great island, which had developed a system of writing long before the Phoenicians, had been in frequent communication with Egypt even before the twelfth dynasty, and had become both politically and artistically the dominant power in the Aegean. It is probable that Egyptian influence goes very far back, and Cretan stone-vase forms recall those of the fourth dynasty. But there is good evidence that bronze was known at any rate at the close of the twelfth dynasty, for at Hagios Onuphrios near Phaistos a bronze dagger and spear-head were found with pre-Mycenaean marble idols and scarabs showing twelfth-dynasty influence. It may therefore be assumed that bronze was known before 2000 B.C., and copper perhaps before the middle of the third millennium. A small series, probably of copper, from Amorgos (on the *right*), comprise spear-heads with openings in the blades for the ligature of the shaft (fig. 118); and in another primitive group, from Thermia (the ancient Cythnos), are examples of the pierced axe (fig. 119) and flat celts with perforation (*a*), already referred to (p. 100). There was no abrupt division between the Cycladic culture and that which was to succeed it; the transition between the two is gradual, and the remains found at Melos and other islands, in the oldest settlements at Mycenae, Tiryns, Athens and elsewhere, prepare the way for the remarkable civilisation of the Mycenaean period.

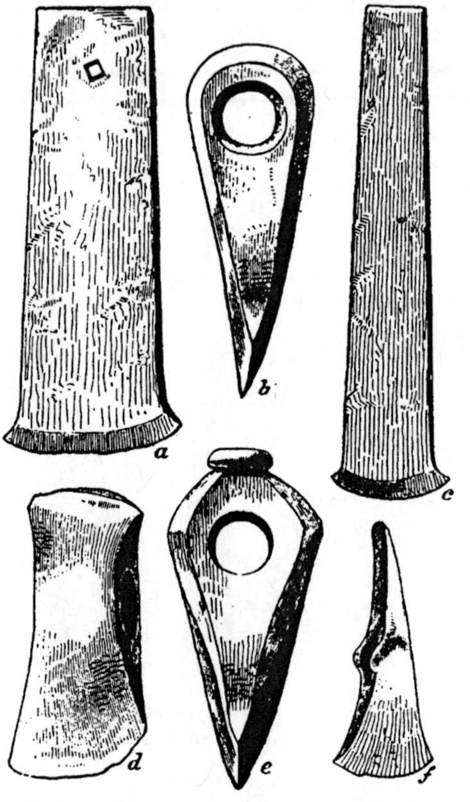

FIG. 119.—Celts and axe-heads, Thermia (Cythnos). ¼

The Mycenaean culture was most widely extended about 1500 B.C., and corresponds in time with the middle and later Bronze age of Europe, the older Aegean period coinciding with the earliest centuries of European metallurgy. The peoples representing these two stages of culture in the Levant are now conjectured to have been neither of Asiatic nor North-European origin, but to have belonged to the same 'Eurafrican' or Mediterranean family which in remoter prehistoric times occupied both the northern and southern shores of the Mediterranean, and spread from the south well into the heart of Europe. They probably spoke non-Aryan languages akin to Lycian and Carian; they are the Pelasgians of the Greek historians and the Keftiu (Cretans) and 'peoples of the sea' of the Egyptian monuments, while the Achaeans and Dorians are successive Aryan invaders from the north. The Achaeans are now thought to have contributed but little to the Mycenaean civilisation which they found existing: that civilisation was therefore neither oriental nor

Greek, but almost entirely due to the genius of the 'Pelasgians,' who, though they borrowed both from Egypt and Babylonia, left upon all that they adopted the impress of their own vigorous individuality.

The name 'Mycenaean' is derived from Mycenae in the plain of Argos, where the most remarkable remains have been found. The principal centres of this civilisation were on the mainland of Greece and in the Aegean islands from Crete to Rhodes; in Asia, apart from the sixth city of Hissarlik (the Homeric Troy), its remains are late and comparatively unimportant, a fact which in itself suffices to weaken any theory of an Asiatic origin. Both Italy and Sicily felt its influence, which from the head of the Adriatic penetrated even into Central and Northern Europe (p. 118). The intercourse of the Mycenaeans with Egypt of the eighteenth and nineteenth dynasties was very close, and it is probable that they actually had settlements in the delta of the Nile. Their pottery has been found at Gurob and Tell el-Amarna (1500–1400.

FIG. 120.—Mycenaean sword, Ialysos, Rhodes. ⅓

B.C.), while contemporary objects, including scarabs, of Amenhetep II, Amenhetep III, Thii, and Amenhetep IV (Khuenaten) have occurred at Mycenae, Ialysos in Rhodes, and in Cyprus. In the Mycenaean period technical skill was very highly developed; metals were inlaid one in another with charming effect; and pottery was turned on the wheel and decorated with painted animals (especially marine) and spiral designs. The precious metals were employed in abundance, and life in the palaces of their kings and princes was marked by a barbaric splendour and opulence. The most striking aspects of this civilisation lie beyond the scope of the present Guide, which must confine itself to the single point of Mycenaean use of industrial metals. The Mycenaeans only knew iron late, and then used it merely for ornaments, such as the finger-rings discovered in the later graves at Mycenae. They cut their timber with bronze axes, and fought with socketed bronze spears and swords (other examples from Ialysos in the First Vase-Room of the Greek and Roman Department, Case A); and it is from one of their sword-types (fig. 120) that the commonest European bronze swords, with hilt and blade cast in one mould, were originally derived. Their weapons were imitated or modified in the north as well as in Sicily and Italy, and their designs were perpetuated in the north-west of the Balkan Peninsula and in Upper Austria down to and

after the early Iron age.   From later graves, dating at least from
the fourteenth century B.C., which in contradistinction to the
earlier or 'shaft-graves' take the form of chambers, often of the
vaulted 'bee-hive' shape, come what seem to be the earliest varieties
of brooch of a simple safety-pin form not unlike the first Italian
examples from Peschiera on the Lake of Garda (p. 113).

Mycenaean civilisation early showed signs of decadence, and
had been superseded for the most part by a culture characterised
by the use of iron and the general adoption of a geometrical style ;
but its disappearance was not simultaneous in all parts of the area
which it covered at the time of its widest distribution, and in
some places it survived considerably longer than in others.

Of the earliest metal culture in parts of Western Asia comparatively little is known, but it is probable that the first

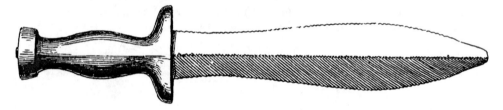

Fig. 121.--Bronze dagger with saw-edge, Crete. ⅓

implements and weapons were of copper, and not of bronze.
Objects from the lowest stratum of the mound at Tell el-Hesy,
near Gaza, have proved to contain no tin; and flat copper celts
resembling Cypriote types have been found in Bethlehem and its
neighbourhood, two rude examples from Beth-Saûr in this Case
containing 99·55 and 99·93 per cent. of copper respectively, with
no trace of tin.   Daggers, also of Cypriote type (as fig. 117), are
known from Bèrût; and bronze axes with almost semicircular
blades and two large holes (in the style of Egyptian weapons
ascribed to the twelfth dynasty) come both from that city and
Northern Syria.   In the latter locality, flat bronze celts, daggers
with bronze hilts, and bronze knives have been discovered not far
from Alexandretta.   It is thus evident that Egyptian and Cypriote
influences were active in Syria, which is just what the history
and geography of this region would lead us to expect.

EGYPT.

It has been stated in the *Stone Age Guide* that palaeolithic
implements have been found in Egypt, and that at the close of
the neolithic period the finest worked flints which are known

were made in that country. The first metal employed was copper, obtained from the mines of the Sinaitic peninsula, to which expeditions were made as early as the time of Semerkhat (first dynasty, about 4300 B.C.) and Tcheser (third dynasty); but copper weapons were already known at the close of the predynastic period. During the first three dynasties (about 4400–3800 B.C.), copper was the only metal, but in the fourth dynasty (about 3766–3600) bronze came into use, whether introduced from Babylonia or not it is impossible to say with certainty. The analyses made by M. Berthelot show that some of the alloys, even in the time of the Ancient Empire, contain as much as 8·2 per cent. of tin, while under the Middle Empire bronze objects contain a proportion exceeding 9 per cent.; indeed, the nature of the alloys used in Egypt seems to have varied very considerably throughout the long period in which bronze was the chief industrial metal. It may be questioned whether the Egyptians were ever absolutely dependent on bronze, for iron was known to them very nearly, if not quite, as early (p. 2), and was easily obtainable both in Egypt itself, Nubia, and the western slopes of Mount Sinai, where it occurs both in haematite and other forms; it is difficult to believe that the people who fashioned objects of haematite at a very early period did not soon discover the useful properties of iron.

Egypt has produced the earliest metal dagger yet known, a copper weapon with two holes for rivets, found at Naqada in a necropolis dating from the period preceding the first dynasty; but the oldest copper daggers from Cyprus and Syria cannot be very much later in date. The rod from Mèdûm, upon which so much depends (p. 9), was found deep down in the filling of a *mastaba* contemporary with the pyramid of Sneferu, and is held to date from the period of that monarch (about 3700 B.C.). Analysis of a complete section gave 8·4 per cent. of tin, while the inner core contained 9·1 per cent. of tin to 89·8 per cent. of copper, with a little arsenic. This is the earliest piece of bronze known, and it will be noticed that the percentage of tin is comparatively high, higher in fact than that of the axes found at Kahun, a site of the twelfth dynasty (about 2500 B.C.), though not quite equal to that of needles from the same place, which contained 10 per cent. Egyptian implements comprise flat axes of various distinctive forms, socketed celts, battle-axes in the form of segments of a circle with two segmental apertures in the blade, straight daggers, knives, gouges, and numerous small objects. Socketed spear-heads apparently come in with the twelfth dynasty, earlier examples having tangs; and though bronze arrow-heads occur in great variety, they seem to be all as late as the New Empire, for the arrow-heads of the earlier period were of flint. Bronze swords of undoubted Egyptian origin are extremely rare. Although

Egypt was in constant communication with Crete, the Aegean Islands, Greece, and Asia Minor, it developed a bronze industry along its own lines, and neither transmitted nor borrowed forms to any great extent. Examples of the characteristic Cypriote form of copper dagger have been found in Egypt, though they do not seem to have been imitated, and the Egyptian type of battle-axe is found in a modified form in south-western Asia. Specimens of the principal types are exhibited in the Third Egyptian Room, Case B, where several interesting inscribed objects may be seen, among others the axes with the prenomens of Kames and Amenhetep II (1600–1500 B.C.). Flint implements continued

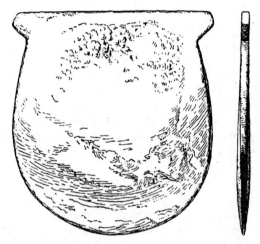

FIG. 122.—Copper axe-head, Abydos, Egypt. $\frac{1}{3}$

to be used in Egypt for a very long period after the introduction of bronze, and some forms of axes occur both in stone and in metal ; for example, the twelfth-dynasty type from Kahun exhibited in Case 152 in the iron gallery. It may be noted that a somewhat similar form is found in Peru (American Room).

On the *East* side of Case J, to the *left*, are a few antiquities from Egypt for comparison, certain of which can be dated with some precision. From Abydos come a copper axe-head and tools of the first or second dynasty (before 4000 B.C.) ; and a copper mirror, adze, chisel, axe-head (fig. 122) of the sixth dynasty (3300–3100), found with a lump of hydrated oxide of iron (not metallic) that, in the opinion of Professor Gowland, was derived from an iron object. A socketed hoe closely resembles examples from Cyprus (Case J) and S. Russia (Case H) ; and a number of arrow-heads from Naucratis, which was founded in the seventh century B.C., belong to the time when iron was in common use.

Case K.

On the *West* side of this Case, besides the Chinese antiquities already dealt with in connection with Siberia (p. 107), are a few objects of importance from Mesopotamia, Persia, and India, to the *right*.

In Babylonia the copper implements (axes, lance-heads, &c.) of Tello go back probably beyond 4000 B.C., the bronze vase of the time of Ur Gur (about 2500) and the bronze statuette of Gudea proving the extreme antiquity of copper, and showing that bronze-working cannot have been introduced very much later than 3000 B.C. (pp. 9 and 118). The discoveries in graves at Mukayyar and Warka (the Biblical Ur of the Chaldees and Erech respectively) throw further light upon metallurgical knowledge at a period estimated between 2500 and 1000 B.C. The graves contained

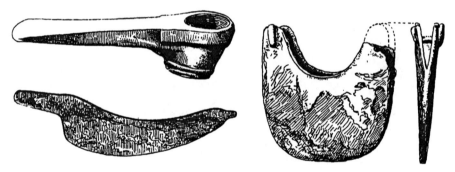

FIG. 123.—Axe-head, knife, and hoe, Tell Sifr, Mesopotamia. ¼

weapons of stone, copper, and bronze; and in some of the latest, iron appears, but is only used for ornamental purposes: lead and gold also occurred in these tombs, but no silver. At Tell Sifr, north of Mukayyar, between the Tigris and the Euphrates, a number of copper or bronze implements and weapons have been excavated. They include axes and adzes with shaft-holes at one end, semi-circular tools split at the butt, straight daggers with riveted tangs, and curved knives; one of the latter on analysis proved to contain no tin. These objects, some of which are in the collection (fig. 123), are said to have been all found together, and are con-jectured to date, if not from the first half of the second millennium, at least from between 1500 and 1000 B.C., a period towards the close of which iron was coming into use. That iron was not generally employed much before the year 1000 B.C. may be assumed from the existence of a bronze sword with a cuneiform inscription, giving the name of an Assyrian king (Adad-nirâri I) of the four-teenth century, as well as from the presence of bronze weapons in the ruins of Nimrud, a city which was only founded about 1300 B.C. But it was evidently introduced within a century or so of the beginning of the first millennium, as an inscription of Tiglath Pileser I, dating from the close of the twelfth century, mentions iron as part of the royal spoils from Commagene, in the north of Syria. It has already been stated (p. 119) that Syria was one of the earliest centres in which iron was worked.

The forms of Babylonian and Assyrian weapons and implements are simple, and there is no attempt at decoration. The swords have only one edge, and socketed celts are absent, though the axes with split butts represent a type from which a socketed celt might easily be derived. The hilts of some daggers resemble Egyptian varieties, a similarity which is easily explained by the intercourse

Fig. 124.—Axe-head, Hamadan (Ecbatana), Persia. ½

existing between the two great oriental monarchies in the time of the eighteenth Egyptian dynasty. Examples of Mesopotamian bronzes may be seen in the Assyrian Room, Cases 26, 27.

The Persian bronze industry was probably influenced in the first instance by Mesopotamia. Axe-heads with shaft-holes and ornamented with lions in relief have been found in the country, and one from Ecbatana is in the collection (fig. 124); tanged spear-heads and other bronze objects were excavated from a mound at Asterabad; and from Khinaman in West Kerman come similar spear-heads, bronze cups, large pins, and a remarkable axe-head, in the ornamental projection of which we may trace the degradation of the lion-design of fig. 124. To judge from their types, and from the reported discovery in association with them of late Greek pottery, these objects must belong to a period when iron had long been in use further to the west. In the district of Lenkoran, on the south-west shore of the Caspian, now Russian territory, M. de Morgan discovered tombs of an early and a late Bronze period, characterized respectively by large cists containing daggers without metal handles, and by small cists in which were found daggers with cast hilts, and long sword-blades. These discoveries bring us to the border of the Caucasian area.

The bronze antiquities of the Caucasus being unrepresented in the collection, little space can be devoted here to the early history of metal-working in that region, which was regarded by the ancients as the seat of metallurgical invention. Its fame was partly due to old traditions like the legend of the Argonauts; partly to the ignorance of geographers, who saw in the great range one of the boundaries of the world; partly, again, to the neighbourhood of tribes like the Tibareni, Moschi (the Tubal and Meshech of the Bible) and Chalybes (p. 8), who worked metal and trafficked with it to foreign countries. But modern research has shown that although some sites are long anterior to the introduction of iron, most of the graves in Caucasian cemeteries, not actually dating from a transitional period, or from a time when iron was well known, must be ascribed to the later and not to the earlier part of the Bronze age. Some archaeologists are inclined to place the majority in the early Iron age, corresponding to what is known as the Hallstatt period in Europe.

Of the sites in Russian Armenia, and on the southern slope of the chain, that at Redkin Lager is among the oldest; and some have ascribed a comparatively early date to the famous cemetery of Koban upon the northern slope, almost midway between the Black and Caspian Seas. On the other hand, it has been pointed out that although bronze weapons largely preponderate over iron on this site, there is an absence of anything like primitive types. Nevertheless, the individuality of many of the forms points to a long period of development, and suggests that a much greater antiquity must be ascribed to their prototypes wherever these may be ultimately found. The brooches with a high bow associated more often with iron, but once or twice with bronze implements at Koban, provide us with an approximate date for the close of the Bronze age in this region. They are of a form common in Greece and Italy, where they are later than the types with an almost straight bow from Mycenae and Peschiera (p. 113). None of them can therefore be older than about the thirteenth century, and those found with iron are probably not far removed in time from the beginning of the first millennium B.C. It may be added that there is a considerable disagreement as to the time when iron was first worked in the Caucasus, some authorities suggesting a period as early as 3000 B.C. The balance of opinion is, however, in favour of a considerably later date.

Mediterranean influence at Koban is evidenced by the frequent occurrence of the spiral; a connection with the south, by the presence of the cowrie (*Cypraea moneta*) of the Persian Gulf, and possibly by the resemblance of certain dagger-hilts to an Assyrian form. A relationship with the lands to the north-east is suggested

by the occurrence of pierced axes resembling examples from
Siberia; and by the discovery in Russian Armenia of an iron
dagger of Siberian type. A connection with east Central Europe
may be inferred from the spiral armlets, penannular collars terminating in spirals, sickles and socketed celts, recalling respectively the later and earlier periods of the Hungarian Bronze age.
Linking as it does two continents and two seas, the Caucasus
naturally assimilated cultural influences from all quarters; and
the Tigris and Euphrates, which rise not far from its southern
borders, must have facilitated early communication with Mesopotamia and the Persian Gulf.

SPAIN AND PORTUGAL.

The most important discoveries made in the Iberian Peninsula are those of MM. Henri and Louis Siret in the district along
the Mediterranean coast between Almeria and Cartagena, where
settlements and tombs dating from the neolithic to the Bronze
age have been brought to light. On the *East* side of the Case, the
neolithic period is represented mainly by shell and other ornaments; the transition period by polished stone implements, flint
flakes and arrow-heads mainly from Campos; and the Bronze age
more fully by remains from El Oficio, Lugarico Viejo, Fuente
Alamo, Zapata and Ifre on the *left*, and El Argar on the *right*. At
the close of the Stone age there appears to have been a time of
transition in which worked flints of great perfection were associated with copper implements, while bronze was still unknown.
The settlements of this period were placed upon low plateaux,
and consisted of groups of boulder-built houses roofed with reeds
and branches; the dead were buried in tombs containing several
bodies. The copper objects comprise flat celts, awls, knives and
saws, and the pottery consists of urns and bowls usually ornamented with incised geometrical designs, and either round or flat
at the base. Some of the transitional sites present features which
indicate external influence probably coming from the East; and
that at Los Millares in the province of Almeria, explored by
M. Louis Siret, is especially remarkable. Here, in addition to
graves of dolmen type, there were chambered tombs with vaulted
roofs, sometimes entered by long passages with lateral cells.
Such tombs, whether constructed, or hewn out of soft rock, can be
traced in their different varieties from the islands of the Western
Mediterranean, through Spain, Portugal, and France (especially
Brittany), to the British Isles and Northern Europe, marking the
course of what is probably the oldest route of intercourse between
East and West. They are generally held to be of oriental deriva-

tion, and many of the objects found in them, or in simpler graves of the same age, confirm this origin. Among these may be mentioned beads of callaïs (a kind of turquoise), objects of carved ivory, and small 'idols' of alabaster, limestone, ivory, or schist, resembling those of pre-Mycenaean period in the islands of the Aegean and at Hissarlik, all of which seem to testify to extended maritime relations. The tombs of Los Millares also yielded beakers of the type found both in Southern and Northern Europe

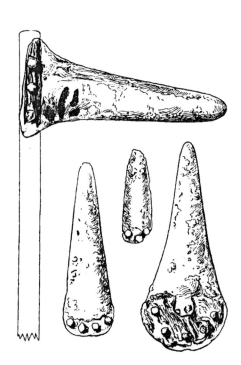

Fig. 125.—Bronze sword El Argar, Almeria. ⅛

Fig. 126.—Halbert, daggers, and knife, El Oficio, Almeria, Spain. ⅓

in the late neolithic or transition period; and these too point to an influence received from without.

During the period in which bronze implements were introduced, the settlements were built on higher and more defensible plateaux, as if the inhabitants lived in fear of attack. The most remarkable is that at El Argar, which is described as a prehistoric citadel. The most characteristic features of this civilisation are the manufacture of pottery (Cases 37–39) peculiarly graceful in design, and the free use of silver. A few stone and flint implements continued to serve for special purposes, such as sharpening knives or mealing grain, but the majority were of copper; and bronze, which was perhaps first known in the form of ornaments, was now also used for weapons.   The commonest arms were daggers, but a primitive form of bronze sword also occurs (fig. 125).   Swords and halberts now appear for the first time, the latter (fig. 126) being also found in North Italy (Case J), North Germany (Case G), and Ireland (Case C).   Silver was used for ornaments as well as for rivets to fasten daggers or halberts to their hafts; its appearance at so early a date is exceptional, and probably to be explained by the presence of very pure ores in the neighbourhood either on or near the surface of the soil.   As a rule, silver is not common until the Iron age, but it is also found in the early graves in the Islands of the Aegean.   The ornaments of the El Argar

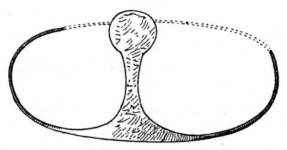

FIG. 127.—Silver diadem, El Argar.   ⅓

period consist of rings, bracelets, and pendants fashioned out of copper, bronze, silver, and occasionally gold, by bending a thick wire into a spiral coil.   Silver diadems, of which seven in all were discovered with interments, form a notable feature (fig. 127). Necklaces were made from beads of bone, ivory, callaïs, serpentine, and various kinds of shells.   The celts are all of primitive type, and well illustrate the advance from the stone pattern to the more slender forms possible in metal (fig. 128).   Arrow-heads of bronze are found; and the awl, familiar in British barrows, was also in use, one specimen remaining in its original bone handle (fig. 129).

The early civilisation revealed by MM. Siret was not entirely confined to the strip of coast between Almeria and Cartagena, but is represented, though on a less remarkable scale, in the other Mediterranean provinces of the south, remains being known from Granada, Cordova, Seville, and elsewhere.   The civilisation of El Argar was followed, whether without intermission it would be difficult to say, by a later development of the Bronze industry in Spain and Portugal, the remains of which are however scanty: its characteristic products are palstaves with two loops, of which examples are shown on the extreme *right* of this Case, while others from Britain are in Case D. There was, in fact, a later Bronze age in Spain as elsewhere, and to this may belong certain cremated remains found in urns in close proximity to unburned skeletons of late neolithic times. These remains were originally

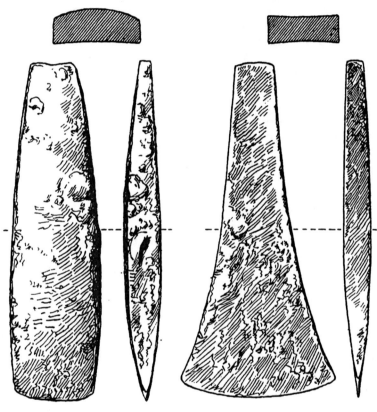

Lugarico Viejo. El Argar.

FIG. 128.—Copper celts, Almeria. ½

FIG. 129.—Awl in bone handle, El Argar. ⅔

attributed by the discoverers to the early transitional period when metallurgy was first introduced; but cremation at such a date would be most abnormal (p. 24), and its occurrence would at once suggest the probability of secondary interments introduced at a later time, and disturbing the original disposition of the graves.   Now that M. Louis Siret has himself expressed doubts as to the accuracy of his earlier theory, his former precise classification has been thrown into some confusion, but an anomaly of an inexplicable kind has been removed.

The metal culture of south-eastern Spain, as represented by the Siret collection, has its origin at a very remote period, when copper gradually appeared side by side with stone.   There are facts which have suggested that bronze was introduced by foreign importation, but however that may be, when once it had obtained a footing, it was worked by local industry, though copper was still retained.   The analogy between Spanish objects and others from the opposite extremity of the Mediterranean, especially from Hissarlik, both in the neolithic age and also in the stage represented by El Argar, would seem to show that even this later period cannot in any case be more recent than 1500 B.C., and may be considerably earlier.   The primitive forms of the implements, and the occurrence of types like the halbert, which are always early (p. 76), may be cited in confirmation of this view.   It may here be repeated that Spain formed a link in the chain of countries connecting the Mediterranean and the North-west in neolithic times, while its wealth in silver and other metals must have early proved an attraction to the peoples of the Mediterranean, even before the time of the Phoenicians. All these facts justify the belief that its inhabitants were among the first to profit by new inventions.   The absence of any elaborate development of the Bronze industry, such as that which we find in Hungary and Scandinavia, goes to prove that the same progressive conditions may have still prevailed when iron came into use.

CONTINENTAL LAKE-DWELLINGS: Case S.

The lake-dwellings of Europe are most perfectly represented on Swiss sites; but though Switzerland is more especially associated with this kind of habitation, it is by no means unique in this respect.   When remains of a like character are found not only all round the Alps but also across Northern Europe; when Herodotus records the existence of similar settlements in Thrace, and Hippocrates of others on the river Phasis; when in various parts of Asia, Africa, and America people are still found dwelling in the same manner, it may be inferred with certainty that the custom of building houses on piles did not result from local or accidental circumstances, but from the universal need for security in unsettled times.   A village in a marsh or lake, and connected with firm ground by a very narrow gangway, was as impregnable as a hill fortress, and certainly more convenient, as it might be extended over a larger area and could never run short of water. So great were these advantages that the obvious drawbacks of such a mode of life counted as nothing in comparison.

The earliest pile-settlements go back to neolithic times, and have been mentioned in the *Stone Age Guide*, where illustrations of modern pile-dwellings in New Guinea will also be found. But in Switzerland the same sites were in continuous occupation throughout, and even after, the Bronze age ; and the occurrence in the same relic-beds of objects dating from consecutive periods and illustrating a gradual cultural development, affords one of the strongest proofs that the civilisation based upon the use of bronze did not come in with fire and sword but rather through gradual immigration and the growth of primitive commerce.

Switzerland and Italy naturally receive more detailed treatment, but we may pass in rapid review the other countries in which lake-dwellings were erected in ancient times. In Savoy, the Lakes of Bourget and Annecy have yielded remains chiefly of the Bronze age. In Bavaria there are several well-known sites : the Lake of Starnberg (Wurmsee), the Mondsee, Attersee, and Fuschlsee have settlements of both the Stone and Bronze ages ; the Neusiedlersee remains of the Stone age only. In Austria-Hungary there is a neolithic site on the Keutschachersee in Carinthia ; while in the Laibacher Moor in Carniola, a large peat-bog now drained, were settlements of both ages, yielding objects which prove Aegean influence, among others conventional human figures of earthen-ware, probably idols, and fine pottery with incised ornament apparently once filled with chalk in a style known both in Cyprus and at Hissarlik (p. 120). In Hungary have been discovered various terremare (p. 101), of very great interest in view of their probable connection with the Italian sites, the most important being that at Lapos Halom near Toszeg, not far from Szolnok on the right bank of the Theiss, where both Bronze and Stone age antiquities have been found. Holland has its *terpen*, which in many respects resembled the terremare, and, like them, have been exploited for agricultural purposes. They are mentioned by Pliny as habitations surrounded by water at high tide ; and the antiquities discovered prove an occupation both in Roman and later times. But as stone implements have also come to light, it seems probable that some of the *terpen* were constructed long before the Romans reached the North Sea.

In addition to the above, there is a whole series of lake-dwellings distributed along Northern Europe from East Prussia to the British Islands, some being regular pile-structures, others the artificial islands strengthened by piles which in Scotland and Ireland are called crannogs. Various eminent authorities, among them Professor Virchow, have held the opinion that these northern settlements belong to the Iron age on account of the numerous objects of late date which their relic-beds contain. It is beyond dispute that many of them were occupied down to mediaeval times, and some have yielded no antiquities earlier than the Iron age. But in others, as for example near Wismar and Bützow in Mecklenburg, in Posen, and East Prussia, stone implements have occurred, the types in some cases being Scandinavian, while occasionally stone and bronze objects have been found together, this confusion of objects belonging to various periods being also characteristic of some Irish and Scottish crannogs. The comparatively frequent occurrence of earlier remains makes it difficult to deny a corresponding antiquity to the sites on which they are found, for it hardly seems possible to ascribe their presence in so many instances to chance alone. In Switzerland itself pile-villages have been found in almost every lake, the small and shallow sheets of water being in many respects the best adapted not only to their erection but also to the preservation of their remains. Since the abandonment of the settlements many of the smaller lakes have been entirely overgrown by peat, so that the pile-dwellings which once stood in water have remained undisturbed in bogs or moors beneath several feet of peat moss, a fact to which we owe much of our knowledge with regard to their constitution and arrangements. In the large lakes only shelving shores were regarded as suitable sites, but even these must have been considerably exposed to wind and rough weather. Most of the settlements were built upon actual piles, but this was not universal, for heaps of stones kept in place by piles were often raised in the lakes, and sometimes, as at Niederwyl in Lake Pfäffikon, the houses were supported by structures of fascines. Many kinds of timber were used, such as oak, beech, elm, birch, ash, fir, elder, maple, poplar, and willow, and the piles were sometimes merely trimmed poles, sometimes split timbers: the latter are considered characteristic of the Bronze age, when the use of metal axes made the carpenter's work easier and more rapid. On the tops of the piles, which were set very close together, wooden platforms were fixed, and on these stood the houses, light structures of wattle covered with clay and thatched with straw, each having as a rule its own hearthstone, and a stone for grinding meal. The settlements often extended several hundred yards along the shore, with which they were connected by means of a gangway ; but canoes were also in general use, several of the dug-out variety (as fig. 148) having been discovered in various sites. It has frequently been found that where a particular site has been occupied during the Stone and Bronze periods, the later settlement is further out in the water than the earlier ; examples of this occur at Möringen and Gerlafingen in the Lake of Bienne, and at Auvernier, Cortaillod, Bevaix, and Estavayer in the Lake of Neuchâtel. The antiquities are found in a blackish stratum of organic *débris* at the base of the piles ; and the charred condition of many of them, as well as of the piles themselves, shows that the majority of the lake-villages were at one time or another destroyed by fire. It is not necessary to suppose that these conflagrations were other than accidental, for all that rose above the level of the water was of an extremely inflammable nature, and the flames, when once fairly kindled, could hardly have been extinguished by the primitive appliances which the inhabitants had at their command.

Many of the Swiss lakes must have been simply fringed with pile-villages, for even now the settlements known to archaeologists

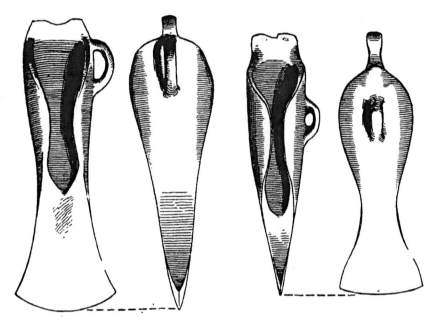

FIG. 130.—Winged celts, Swiss lake-dwellings. ½

are thickly dotted round their shores: thus, Lake Neuchâtel has more than thirty, while some fifty are scattered round the Lake of Constance. In the majority of cases both stone and bronze antiquities are found, but some settlements, like that at Schachen on Lake Constance, belong almost exclusively to the Bronze age. In others, as at Vinelz in the Lake of Bienne, and St. Blaise in the Lake of Neuchâtel, a period of transition from stone to metal is clearly marked ; the metal axes are of early types, while some daggers from St. Blaise closely resemble the usual flint forms. The fact that the majority of these early metal objects are of copper has its bearing on the discussion as to the existence of a Copper stage of culture preceding that of Bronze (p. 6). It is impossible to enumerate the various stations remarkable for the bronze objects which they have yielded; but special mention may be made of the pile city at Morges on the Lake of Geneva, where the Bronze age settlement was some $1,200 \times 150$ ft. in extent, and yielded antiquities important alike for their number and high artistic quality.

The principal bronze objects discovered in the lake-dwellings are celts (the 'winged' type like fig. 130 predominating, but the flat, flanged and socketed types are all present); dagger-blades with rivets for attachment to perishable hilts now lost; knives with curved blades (fig. 131), frequently ornamented, and either with tangs, sockets, or solid handles cast in one piece; swords with flat handles, pierced for rivets, or complete with hilts cast in the round, a few of the latter from Lake Luissel, Canton

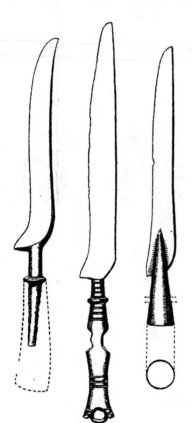

FIG. 131.—Knives, Swiss lake-dwellings. ⅓

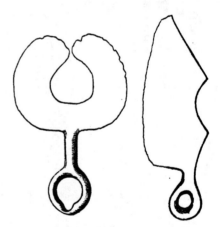

FIG. 132.—Razors, Swiss lake-dwellings. ½

de Vaud, terminating in 'antennae' (cf. fig. 110) which persisted into the early Iron age; razors of peculiar form (fig. 132): sickles (like fig. 67, Taplow); chisels (fig. 133); gouges; socketed hammers; saws; fish-hooks (fig. 134); horse-bits; vessels and dishes; rivets and nails; tweezers and needles; armlets and bracelets (solid and hollow); finger-rings; pendants; buttons; long hair-pins (very common); and brooches of various safety-pin types (rare). Gold is rarely met with, and then only in the form of small objects such as beads, earrings, and finger-rings; but tin occurs in the form of ingots as well as of ornaments, and fine earthenware vessels were decorated with strips of it.

Of stone objects which continued to be used in this period may be mentioned: hearthstones; sharpening-stones; mealing-stones for grinding grain; arrow-heads; finely-made pierced axe-hammers; moulds for making implements; pierced sinkers and discoidal stones, said to have been used by potters for finishing the bases of vessels. Doubtless flakes and scrapers, and even

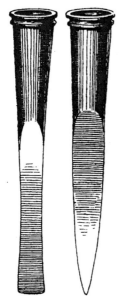

Fig. 133.—Socketed chisel, Swiss lake-dwelling.

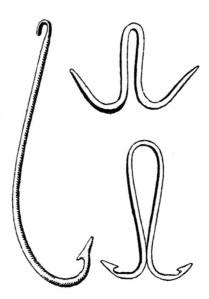

Fig. 134.—Fish-hooks, Swiss lake-dwellings.

flint knives and saws, were also used, though more and more rarely as time went on.

Stag-horn and bone were in less demand for tools than during the Stone age, but were still employed for various purposes, such as making the side-pieces of horse-bits, for fish-spears, and barbed harpoon-heads. All kinds of things were made of wood, from dug-out canoes, oars. house-doors, boxes, and yew bows, to dishes, ladles, and combs.

Pottery was of two sorts: a rougher kind containing sand and grit, and a ware of finer composition, sometimes of a dark grey colour, or blackened with graphite or charcoal. Pottery of this latter class was, even in the neolithic period, ornamented with deeply incised designs inlaid with a white chalky substance, a circumstance which, like the occurrence of the small idols at Laibach, suggests a cultural connection with the Eastern Mediterranean. The ornament is geometrical, consisting of impressed or incised circles, semicircles, triangles, dots, zigzags and herring-bone bands. A rare method of decoration by means of applied strips of tin was practised at the settlements of Cortaillod, Corce-lettes, and Estavayer, on the Lake of Neuchâtel, as well as in the lakes of Savoy (fig. 135). The forms include jugs, bowls, dishes, vases, plates, and beakers. Some of the vessels are pointed at the base, and cannot stand upright unless supported by clay rings, of which numerous examples have been found. Other objects of earthenware are crucibles, clay spindle-whorls, and loom-weights. Textiles are represented by flax-cloth, yarn, thread,

FIG. 135.—Vase with applied tin, Conjux, Lake of Bourget. ½

and netting. The inhabitants of the lake-dwellings were ac-quainted with numerous animals, many of which were domesti-cated. The following list will give some idea of the variety of animal remains discovered : *wild animals*—bison, aurochs, urus, elk, stag, roe-deer, great bear, wild boar, fox, wild-cat, marten, pole-cat, beaver, otter, badger, hare, squirrel, field-mouse ; *domes-ticated animals*—horse, cow, sheep, goat and dog. Among birds may be mentioned the stork, heron, sea-gull, wild-duck and teal ; and among fish and reptiles, the tortoise, frog, toad, carp, pike and salmon. Vegetable remains include wheat and barley (often found in carbonised masses), flax, raspberries, blackberries, straw-berries, apples, sloes, hazel and beech nuts.

From the nature of the above remains it is possible to construct a picture of the kind of life led by the people of the pile-dwellings. They were still hunters and fishermen, but their flocks and herds and their fields of corn provided them with food obtained without exertion or danger. They rode horses and drove wagons or chariots, as is proved by the discovery of numerous bits and several wooden wheels; this point is of interest because these bits and wheels are the first certain evidence of the domestication of the horse. The crucibles, moulds, ingots and pieces of slag and scoriae, show that they had a knowledge of metallurgy, and made their implements and weapons themselves. The spindle-whorls, loom-weights, and pieces of cloth, often very finely made, are sufficient evidence that they were skilful weavers. Though they were such capable potters, there is no evidence that they knew of the potter's wheel. Their artistic faculty was not highly developed, and, unlike the ancient cave-dwellers of Southern France who were able to reproduce animal forms with vigour and accuracy, they did not advance beyond geometrical designs of a simple description. That they had, like all peoples in their stage of culture, a love of personal adornment we know from the large numbers of beads, rings, armlets, pendants, &c., which the investigation of their settlements has disclosed (examples in Case from Lake of Bourget in Savoy). They had various weapons for close quarters, and used javelins and yew bows for attacking at a distance. Of their moral and intellectual qualities nothing can be said; but the character of various remains discovered on the sites of their settlements indicates that they had some kind of religious cult. Among these 'ceremonial' objects may be cited some bronze tubes with appended rings (p. 28), which can hardly have a practical use, and recall the *sistra* or rattles of a somewhat similar kind shaken during religious ceremonies in Japan. Rings found at Morges, Thonon, resembling armlets, but incurved at the back and inconvenient to wear, may, it is thought, have served the same purpose as the *armilla sacra* which the ancient Germans held in the hand when taking a solemn oath. Then there are clay figures of animals, the little earthenware 'idols,' and certain horned objects of pottery or wood, which, if not put to practical use, may have been connected with a primitive form of cult.

The mention of these objects leads by a natural transition to the question of intercourse between Central Europe and the outer world. As might be expected, the method of ornamenting pottery by inlaying incised designs with chalk is found at Hissarlik and in Cyprus in prehistoric times; the presence of amber beads suggests intercourse with the Baltic; while brooches and other objects, both of Scandinavian and North Italian affinities, show that the countries to north and south exerted some influence on the intervening territory. The quantity of jade implements discovered in the Swiss lakes is held by some to prove that even in the Stone age communication must have existed with the East.

Human remains have been found in many of the lake sites, though complete skeletons are rare, and have evidently not been intentionally placed in the positions in which they were found.

For a long time the manner in which the dead were disposed of remained a problem to the explorers of the pile-settlements; but light was thrown upon this point by the discovery in 1876, on the mainland opposite the settlement of Auvernier, of a tomb or vault surrounded and covered by large slabs of stone and containing the remains of about 120 bodies, the skulls of which were identical in character with those actually found under water among the piles. The chamber formed by these flags was 5 ft. 3 in. × 3 ft. 8 in. and 5 ft. 10 in. deep, and the bodies were probably placed in a sitting position round the sides: the implements found were of both stone and bronze, so that the interment may be ascribed to the transition period. There were smaller supplementary tombs near the larger chamber, one containing human remains; and not far off was the skeleton of a child without any stone cist. In the same and the following year similar discoveries were made near Montreux, with relics chiefly of the Bronze age; and in 1884 other Bronze age tombs came to light in the same locality. Cist-interments also occurred at Morges; and at St. Prex a cemetery was found in which the skeletons had been simply placed in the earth, the ornaments associated with them belonging to the most highly developed period of Bronze age art. Amongst these free burials were cinerary urns which resembled the lake-dwelling pottery of the Bronze age, containing bones and charcoal, and showing that inhumation and incineration were practised concurrently.

The craniological investigations of which these remains have been the subject are held to prove that the lake-dwellers originally belonged to the short-headed Alpine race which is still so clearly represented among the Swiss population, but that there was a gradual increase of long-headed people who already predominated during the later Bronze age. Professor Virchow was of opinion that the new elements were introduced by slow degrees, and his contentions are supported by remains of dwellings and implements which show no traces of sudden or fundamental modifications until the beginning of the Iron age. The greater part of the objects in the Case were obtained from the Lakes of Neuchâtel and Bienne in Switzerland, and from the Lake of Bourget in Savoy. A full account of the pile-settlements will be found in Dr. Robert Munro's book *The Lake-Dwellings of Europe*.

LAKE-DWELLINGS IN THE BRITISH ISLES.

The greater number of these habitations must be ascribed to the Iron age, and as such do not come within the scope of the present Guide; but stone and bronze antiquities which have been found in several of them, suggest that these at least were occupied at an earlier period. On any other supposition these objects must either have been accidentally dropped into the water over these precise spots, before the dwellings were constructed, or else deposited at a time when iron was already in use. It is in the highest degree improbable that the presence of these weapons and implements can be due to chance, while the supposition that they were still in use in the Iron age is equally unsatisfactory. For although at a time of transition the old material may persist by the side of the new, implements of *two* earlier periods would hardly survive into a third, as would be the case, for example, if the lake-dwellings at Holderness in Yorkshire were ascribed to the Iron age, as here both stone and bronze implements have been discovered. Stone moulds for casting bronze spear-heads are known from crannogs in Lough Gur (fig. 53), Co. Limerick, and Lough Scur, Co. Leitrim; and bronze celts and daggers from Lake Monalty and Lough-na-Glack in Co. Monaghan.

Although these facts point to an occupation of these sites in the neolithic and Bronze ages, it is undoubted that the British lake-dwellings as a class are connected with the Iron age, since the majority of the antiquities yielded by exploration belong to that period. The Irish and Scottish crannogs continued in occupation right through the Middle Ages. Historical records make mention of them; and the crannog of Lough Lane, Roscommon, was taken by assault by Sir R. Bingham in the reign of Queen Elizabeth. In view of these facts the description of British lake-dwellings here given will be confined within the narrowest possible limits.

A crannog (derived from *crann*, a tree) is an artificial island usually made of logs laid transversely, with the addition of brushwood, stones, and earth, and surrounded by one or more stockades, the piles of which were held together by branches of trees or even by mortised beams. It was often surmounted by a platform of timbers on which the hearthstone was placed and the wattle-and-daub huts erected, and was generally oval or circular with a diameter of at least 60 or 70 feet. There was a gangway of some kind connecting it with the shore, but the occupants were invariably supplied with dug-out canoes. of which numerous examples have been found (as fig. 148). The above method of construction seems to have been most frequently adopted where the bottom of the lake was soft and yielding; in the rarer cases when it was hard and rocky the artificial island was formed by piling up stones until the surface of the water was reached. Crannogs are most numerous in Ireland and Scotland, those in the counties of Ayr, Dumfries, and Wigtown having proved archaeologically the most valuable, but they are also known in England and Wales. The most striking English examples are perhaps those excavated by Mr. Thomas Boynton in 1880, at Holderness in Yorkshire, where, as has been already stated, both stone and bronze implements were found.

The lake-dwellings of these islands were not, however, confined to the crannog type. At Barton Mere, near Bury St. Edmunds, the huts had been built on piles, after the Central European manner, and here socketed bronze spear-heads occurred. Other pile-dwellings have been explored at Newbury in Berks., Southwark and London Wall in the Metropolis, and at Glastonbury, but these are chiefly of too late a date for treatment in a Guide confined to the Bronze age.

MOREL COLLECTION: FRANCE.

In the southern or Gaulish wing of the Central Saloon, on the way to the Gold Ornament Room, is arranged the collection

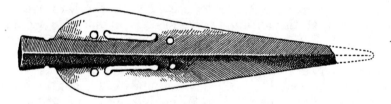

Fig. 136.—Spear-head with pierced blades, France. ⅓

formed by M. Léon Morel, of Rheims. In Table-case N is a series of bronze swords with chapes either tapering like fig. 14, or of the winged type (fig. 15), in exaggerated form. The latter belong to the Hallstatt period, and that from Joncquières, Vaucluse, has a width of 9¼ in. Attention should also be directed to the objects found with the sword at Courtavant, Aube, and to the curved mark of the scabbard-mouth on the blade.

In Wall-cases 75, 76, on the main shelf, are other antiquities of the Bronze age from this collection, all being from the Champagne district or the Lower Rhone, except two primitive copper daggers of a well-known form from Cyprus (like fig. 117). A small series of celts contains examples of most of the French forms, and are arranged in their probable chronological order, beginning on the left. On the back slope with other specimens, on a board, may be seen a peculiar spear-head with circular holes and slits in the blades (fig. 136), and an example of a British or Irish type of lance-head, with loops on the socket.

GOLD ORNAMENT ROOM.

There is no doubt that gold was known in some parts of Europe in the neolithic period, and it may possibly have been the first metal worked in this part of the world. It was obtained abundantly in four centres: (i) Macedonia, Thrace, and Thasos; (ii) Hungary and Transylvania; (iii) Spain; and (iv) Ireland, the mineral wealth of the Ural mountains not being accessible at

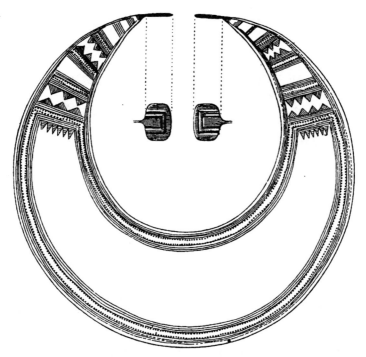

FIG. 137.—Gold collar, Llanllyfni, Carnarvonshire. ⅓

that early date. Gold objects dating from the Bronze age are generally of native metal (alloyed with silver), and are mostly ornamental, though several ponderous axe-heads of the precious metal have been found in Transylvania. The collection here is mainly from the British Isles, and a peculiar interest attaches to the crescent-shaped ornaments, sometimes called *lunulae* (fig. 137), which are undoubtedly of Irish origin. They were worn on the neck, and not as diadems on the heads, and are of very rare occurrence on the Continent, examples from France (Depts. Manche, Côtes-du-Nord, and Vendèe) and Denmark (Zealand and Fünen) showing intercourse with Ireland either by way of Britain or more probably direct by sea. Ships carved on the rocks of Sweden as well as at New Grange and Dowth, Co. Meath, and Gavr'inis, Morbihan, would in themselves indicate extensive navigation ; and attention has already been directed to various objects of the early Bronze age imported from these islands into Scandinavia. Irish gold may have been bartered for amber from Jutland, but amber was also found on our own east coast, and may have been sufficient for the local demand. Irish gold seems to have been in general use quite early in the Bronze age, for the crescents, of which over 30 are preserved

FIG. 138.—Gold armlet, Brahalish, Bantry, Co. Cork. $\frac{2}{3}$

at Dublin, show an early type of ornament, and two specimens have been found in Cornwall with a bronze (or copper) celt of primitive form.

The greater part of the gold ornaments exhibited comes from Ireland, but very few pieces have any history, and the archaeological value of the series is thereby impaired. It is significant that many of the gold-finds in England have been in the south-west, while Wales, also within easy reach of Ireland, has also been productive. The metal was not confined to any one district in Ireland, but was found or traded all over the island, which has been regarded as the El Dorado of the ancient world. According to M. Salomon Reinach, this industry of the Iberian population was ruined by a foreign invasion about 1000 B.C., and some Keltic-speaking barbarians (possibly the Goidels) arrested the development of Ireland till the advent of more invaders some time before 200 B.C., when the Late Keltic culture was introduced.

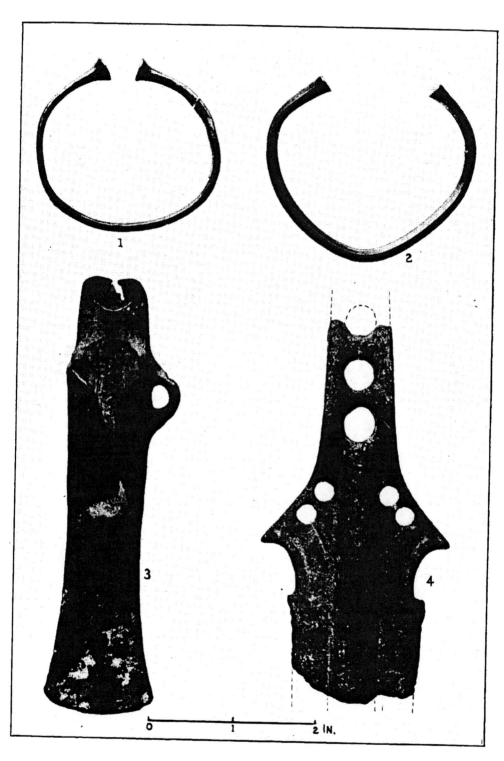

PLATE IX. CELT, SWORD, AND GOLD BRACELETS, BEACHY HEAD, SUSSEX.
(Case C, and Gold Ornament Room, *see* pp. 78, 88.)

Gold Ornament Room, Case J.

To the *left* are Irish specimens, including bracelets of a peculiar type with hollow conical or cup-shaped terminals (fig. 138); and forms intermediate between these and the small dress-fasteners, showing some connection between them, though the exact use of many pieces is still obscure. A cup-shaped end is sometimes seen on bronze pins in Ireland (p. 27) and abroad, while the ends of the dress-fasteners are flat, though not in the same plane. The central

FIG. 140.—Gold fragment,
Mountfield, Sussex.

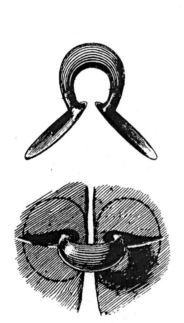

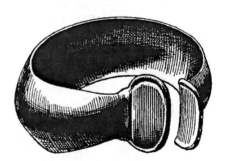

FIG. 139.—Gold clasp for the
dress, Ireland. ⅔

FIG. 141.—Gold bracelet,
Tisbury, Wilts. ⅔

limb, which alone was visible if Sir William Wilde's theory as to their use (fig. 139) is correct, is always striated longitudinally; and in some cases the bow of the Scandinavian spectacle-brooch (fig. 111) has the same decoration, while its size and shape are in close agreement. It is conceivable that the idea was imported from Denmark or Sweden between the ninth and seventh century B.C. Part of a rich hoard found at Newmarket-on-Fergus, Co. Clare, is here shown, consisting of bracelets of a simple character, and a large series of penannular pieces commonly known as 'ring-money.' Gold rings and bracelets of the true Bronze period are often of thin strands like wire, while the thick and heavy ring-money is

in Scandinavia referred to the early Iron age, after 500 B.C.
Many pieces present a surface of gold and silver in alternate rings,
and a certain number have a core of baser metal (copper or iron)
concealed by a thin coating of gold.   The Mountfield fragments
(fig. 140) may be parts of bracelets, and several patterns are represented in the find at Morvah, Cornwall.   A rare form for England
has been found with others at Tisbury, Wilts. (fig. 141, cf. p. 39),

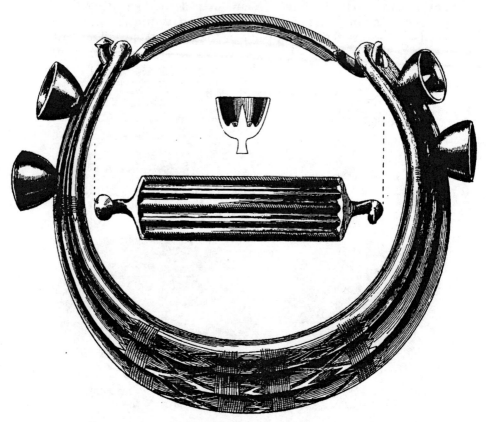

FIG. 142.—Gold collar, Cintra, Lisbon.   ⅔

and is temporarily shown, with other antiquities bequeathed by
Sir Wollaston Franks, in the passage leading to this room
(second metal Case on the *right*).

Of foreign examples the most important is the splendid collar from
Cintra (fig. 142), which resembles in form the triple bronze collars
of Scandinavia attributed to the seventh or sixth century, while
the four cup-shaped projections are a feature of the Hallstatt
period and occur on the pommel of a bronze sword from Whitting-
ham, Northumberland.   The collar may therefore be assigned to
about the eighth century B.C.   Spiral coils of wire, possibly a form

of ring-money, are shown from Italy and Spain : the former with a bulla of about the first century B.C., and the latter with ornaments from the grave of a child. The two gold torcs of Gaulish origin belong definitely to the La Tène period (Iron age).

Gold Ornament Room, Case K.

At the back of the Case is a piece of gold armour (plate x) formerly known as the Mold corslet, but now seen to be a peytrel (French, *poitrail*) or brunt for a pony. It is mounted on a copper

FIG. 143.—Mold pey-
trel on pony.

FIG. 144.—Gold torc, Boyton,
Suffolk. ½

plate as originally worn, fragments of the lining being shown at the side ; and was found just seventy years ago with a man's bones in a cist which had been covered with three or four hundred loads of pebbles and other stones, forming a cairn called Bryn-yr Ellyllon (Hill of the Fairies or Goblins), near the river Alun at Mold, Flintshire. There were also in the cist many amber beads and remains of coarse cloth, which had been fastened round the edges of the peytrel as a fringe (fig. 143). Traces of iron are also said to have been noticed, and two or three yards from the spot was found a cinerary urn. A romantic story is also told of the discovery, which has been attributed to second-sight ; and several pieces, including the gold straps for fastening, were lost after the peytrel had been thrown aside as worthless. Several of these pieces have been recovered, and presented at intervals by various donors. The depth at the centre (8½ in.) can be exactly determined, as the upper and lower borders (in which are holes for attaching the fringe) are still preserved ; and the present length is about 3 ft. 7 in., but it is not complete at either end. The size is well adapted for a pony of about twelve hands, like the famous Welsh breed of the present day. The thin gold plate is embossed in

FIG. 145 —Gold bracelet with ring-money, Ely, Cambs.

a style resembling that seen on the bucklers from Wales and elsewhere (Cases 3, 4, 6, 7) ; but a richer variety of patterns is here employed, consisting of circular bosses of two sizes, pyra-midal rivet-heads, pointed ovals, and other bosses of quadrangular shape, separated by simple raised lines. It was probably not earlier than the shields, and the presence of iron may indicate even a later date. A discovery of this kind demonstrates in a striking manner the abundance of gold at the end of our Bronze period. It is obvious that before a warrior would decorate his horse with the precious metal, he had doubtless satisfied his own personal needs in this direction.

The crescent necklets in this Case have been already referred to (p. 145).

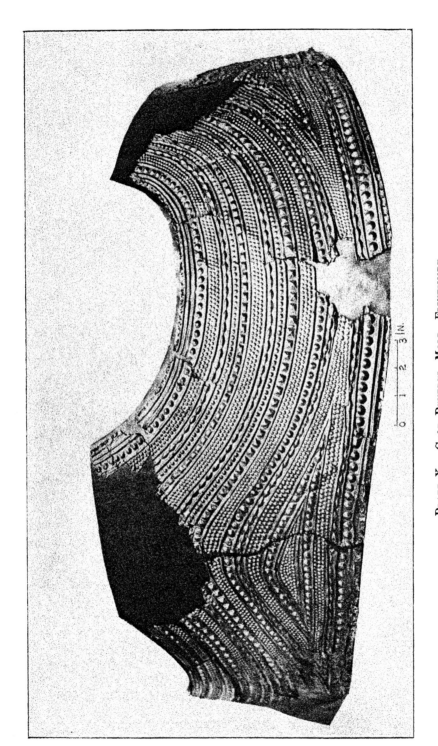

PLATE X. GOLD PEYTREL, MOLD, FLINTSHIRE.
Go d Ornamen Room *see* p. 49.

Gold Ornament Room, Case L.

Collars and armlets of twisted metal (Latin, *torquis*), the fastening being either a pair of simple hooks or long bars thickening towards the end and interlocking. At the junction of the torc illustrated from Suffolk (fig. 144) is seen a piece of ring-money, as also on a larger specimen from Lincolnshire, while a bracelet (fig. 145) with six such pieces, found with part of a bronze rapier, is shown in this Case. The twisting of the metal was no doubt to give

Fig. 146.—Bronze sun-disc, Ireland. ⅔

brilliancy to the ornament, and is characteristic of the transition between the Bronze and Iron periods; but further particulars are wanted for a more precise chronology.

In the front of the Case are four gold discs and one of bronze, the significance of which has been verified by a recent discovery in Denmark. At Trundholm, in the north of Zealand, an engraved bronze disc, 6 in. in diameter, covered with gold foil, has been found mounted on a miniature carriage drawn by a horse. This was undoubtedly a ceremonial object, and connected with sun-worship, so that the discovery of more than one such disc (fig. 146) in Ireland shows the extent of the cult before the first millennium B.C., the Danish example being dated by Dr. Sophus Müller before the year 1000 B.C. Intentional damage had been done to the disc and car before deposit in the Trundholm moss, and they may be regarded as a votive offering. A damaged disc with gold covering

has been found in Ireland; and that here illustrated has been
broken across the centre. The ornament on those from Ireland
is if anything later, and does not include the spiral (p. 96). The
bronze disc has lugs on the margin exactly in the same position
as in the Danish example, the lower one being for the purpose of
fixing the disc to the axle of the carriage, the other for holding the
horse's rein (fig. 147). It lacks, however, the gold plate, which was
no doubt pressed into the pattern; and the Irish gold discs were

Fig. 147.—Sun-disc on model carriage.   ½

probably fixed to a bronze foundation. The cruciform pattern on
two of them is a well-known solar symbol, and the other two may
well have been intended to represent the sun.

Portico: Canoes.

Under the portico, on the east, outside the Hall door, are three
'dug-out' canoes which probably date from the Bronze period.
They belong to a common type, formed out of a tree-trunk split
lengthwise, the work of excavating the interior being performed
by tools of stone or bronze, and possibly by fire. The largest of
the three (fig. 148) was found in 1834 in a drain which probably
represents an ancient course of the Arun between North and
South Stoke, the exact site being about 150 yards from the
present stream. It is about 35 ft. long, nearly 2 ft. deep, 4½ ft.
wide in the middle, and 4½ in. thick at the bottom. Three bars
across the bottom inside gave additional strength, and also served
as a foothold for the crew, but the mode of propulsion is uncertain. Another was found during excavations for the Royal Albert

Dock at North Woolwich, 1878. The oak trunk was carefully worked, the bottom and sides being flat and rectangular; but there are no signs of keel, stretchers or rowlocks. Both ends were alike, straight and somewhat raised, and the length was 17 ft. with a beam of about 2 ft. It was found on the bank of a stream which had cut its way through a bed of peat. The third is also of oak, nearly 15 ft. in length, and 2 ft. 4 in. wide: the ends both rounded, and the sides almost at right angles to the flat bottom. On the right side of the stern a hole had been drilled vertically through the gunwale for a peg, but the corresponding part of the left gunwale is wanting. A pole, perhaps used for punting, was lying under the boat which was itself 6 feet from the surface on an ancient bank of the Lea at Walthamstow.

Though 'dug-out' canoes are frequently found, and are still in use in many parts of the world, no metal objects are known to have been found in association with any excavated in our islands. In one of several found on the site of Glasgow lay a polished celt of greenstone, and their position in a marine formation about 25 feet above the present level of the sea points to a considerable upheaval of this part of Scotland in recent geological times.

Fig. 148.—Dug-out canoe, South Stoke, Sussex.

INDEX

Abauj, 100.
Abercromby, Hon. John, 24.
Abingdon, Berks., 76.
Abruzzi, 86, 116, 117
Abydos, Egypt, 126.
Achaeans, 122.
Acklam, East Riding of Yorkshire, 16.
Adalia, 119.
Adige, River, 95.
Adriatic, 95, 123
Adzes, 126, 127.
Aegean culture, 89, 100, 106, 112, 117.
Aeschylus, 7.
Africa, 4.
Alaw, River, 31.
Albert Dock, Royal, 152.
Aldbourne, Wilts , 60, 63.
Almeria, 66, 130.
Alpine race, 15, 142.
Alps, 116, 117.
Alwinton, Northumberland, 58.
Amber, 12, 29, 62, 91–3, 95, 103, 116, 141, 146, 149.
Amenhetep, 26, 123, 125.
Amerden, Bucks, 37.
America, 4, 10, 66, 79, 86.
Amorgos, 117, 121, 122.
Analyses, 6, 27, 29, 59, 68, 124, 125.
Anderson, Dr. Joseph, 36.
Anglesey, 32, 34, 92.
Animals, domestic, 140.
— wild, 140.
Annam, 108.
'Antennae' sword, 105.
Anvils, 72, 88, 89.
Appleford, Berks., 52.
Aps, Ardèche, 87.
Argyllshire, 79.
Armenia, 129.
Armlets, 75, 84, 85, 88, 92, 97, 100, 138, 151.
Arreton Down, I. W., 73, 81.
Arrow-heads, 106, 109, 113, 126, 132.
Arun, River, 152.
Aryans, 12–15, 24, 122.
Ashford, Middlesex, 46, 49.
Asia Minor, 66.
Athlone, Co. Westmeath, 80.
Atkinson, Rev. J. C., 17.

Austria-Hungary, 99, 113, 135.
Auvergne, 88.
Auvernier, 142.
Avebury, Lord, 23.
Avignon, 89.
Awls, 59, 60, 62, 84, 120, 130, 132, 133.
Axe-adzes, 100.
Axe-hammers, stone, 74, 92–94, 113, 119.
Axes, 107, 109, 113, 128, 145.

Babylonia, 6.
Badbury Rings, Dorset, 78.
Ballymenach, Argyllshire, 64.
Baltic, 106.
Bamborough, Northumberland, 55, 58.
Bargia Verezzi, 66.
Barrows, 16, 42, 89.
Barrows, contents of, 18, 19, 89.
Barry, Sir F. Tress, 34.
Barton Mere, Suffolk, 144.
Bateman, Thos., 17.
Battersea, London, 84.
Battle, Sussex, 30.
Battle-axes, 100, 101, 125.
Bavaria, 113.
Beachy Head, Sussex, 78, 88.
Beads, 60, 62, 91–94, 96, 132, 138:
Beakers (drinking-cups), 44, 65, 111, 112, 119, 120, 131.
Beckhampton, Wilts., 61.
Beech-tree, 13.
Beedon, Berks., 50.
Beitzsch, 97.
Belgae, 16, 22.
Bells, 28.
Belt, 102
Berne Museum, 120.
Berry Head, Devon, 48.
Berthelot, M., 125.
Bethlehem, 124.
Beth-Saûr, 124.
Beverley, East Riding of Yorkshire, 79, 80, 88.
Bienne, Lake of, 136, 137.
Biskra, 66.
Boar's tusk, 63.
Bohuslän, 31, 104

Bone ornament, 93.
Bones of animals, 43, 50, 53, 56, 63, 109, 140.
Borlase, Mr., 47.
Bourget, Lake of, 135, 140.
Bowls, 64, 92, 109, 120, 130, 140.
Bows, 139, 141.
Boxes, 105.
Boyton, Suffolk, 149.
Bracelets, 86, 87, 106, 119, 120, 132, 138, 147, 150.
Bracers, 52, 90, 93, 95.
Bradley, Derbyshire, 92.
Brahalish, Co. Cork, 146.
Brandon, Suffolk, 52, 93, 95.
Brenner Pass, 95.
Bridlington, East Riding of Yorkshire, 92.
Brighton, Sussex, 74, 93.
Brigmerston Down, Wilts., 84
Britons, 42.
Brittany, 85, 87, 88, 90.
Brixham, Devon, 47.
Brixworth, Northants, 52.
Broadward, Shropshire, 39, 85.
Brochs, 34.
Bromley-by-Bow, Essex, 39
Bronwen the Fair, 31.
Bronze age, 1.
Brooches, 87, 97, 105, 106, 112, 113, 115, 116, 124, 129, 138, 141.
Broughton, Hants, 52.
— Lincolnshire, 49.
Brynmor-Jones, Mr., 21.
Bryn-yr Ellyllon, Flintshire, 149.
Brythons, 15, 22.
Buckel-urnen, 64.
Bucklers, 30, 150.
Buda-Pesth, 65, 120.
Bulford, Wilts., 51.
Burial, primary, 56, 74, 104.
— secondary, 56, 104.
Burma, 108.
Burton Fleming, East Riding of Yorkshire, 94.
Bury St. Edmunds, Suffolk, 144.
Butmir, 106, 118.
Butterwick, East Riding of Yorkshire, 40, 59, 117.

OXFORD: HORACE HART
PRINTER TO THE UNIVERSITY

CPSIA information can be obtained at www.ICGtesting.com
Printed in the USA
LVOW07s1355141215

466588LV00015B/360/P